STYLE SCHOOL

エスエス

GREETINGS FROM  STYLE SCHOOL

STYLE SCHOOL NAVIGATOR
CHARACTER DESIGN: YUTAKA MIZUTANI

S Esumi
Illustration-loving
high school student

S-Model Mark Zero (a.k.a. S-"O")
Picture-drawing robot from the future

 Hello, everyone! Thanks for picking up *Style School*. I'm your navigator, S Esumi.

 And I'm your navigator, S-Maru. We've been summoned here for the inaugural issue of this new magazine!

 First, let us introduce ourselves. I'm a high school student, but I love illustration and I've just started drawing myself. I hope I can get really good at it . . .

 I'm a picture-drawing robot, "S-Model Mark Zero." "Zero" because I'm a prototype, and 0 looks like "O" so they call me "S-O." My body is equipped with every kind of art implement available, and there's a palette of rainbow colors on my chest. All I do is press a button to change the images in the palette and change them to real art supplies.

 . . .

 Uhh...? You still with me?

 A "picture-drawing robot". . . ? That's totally unrealistic! How are the readers supposed to get used to their navigator if he's gonna be so hard to believe?

 Say what?! Are you denying my very existence on page one?!

 Aw, forget about it . . . I'll make up for it somehow.

 "Make up for it"?! So, S, are *you* gonna draw the pictures?

 . . .

 I came here from the 22nd century to help you, because you can't draw so well. So we can draw pictures together.

 "Came from the future" sounds kinda old-fashioned for some reason . . .

 In the 22nd century—2190 to be precise—Japan hasn't changed very much since today. Of course, science has advanced, but people's tastes and trends in illustration are the same as they are now. People are still using pens and paint in the 22nd century. Everything isn't being done with CG. That's why I came back to Japan in this era, when illustration was really taking off. I came looking for art materials and to see various illustrating techniques to further the development of illustration in the future!

 So why did you come to *me*?

 I can't tell you that yet, but I figured I'd start my illustration collection with you to begin with, S, just like if you were conquering the world, you'd start with an assault on a nearby kindergarten first.

 That's a sick example! But I want to see lots of beautiful illustrations, too, and I'm really keen to learn all kinds of different drawing styles. So I'll try my hardest!

 Cool!

 Anyway, *Style School* is a "How-to & Art" magazine, so the book is divided into instructional sections and showcase sections.

 The first issue of *Style School* shows you how to make the art that appeared in our sister magazine, *S*. A lot of people wanted to know how the art in that issue was created, and now we're pleased to show you exactly how!

 That's right. Like in the How-To on Imperial Boy (see page 36), I was surprised how well I understood the construction of such a complicated illustration once I saw what happened behind the scenes.

 And, readers, if there are any other artist's working techniques you'd like to know about, let us know. We'd love to hear from you!

 Now the art pages—these were a big surprise! How did we end up with submissions from Taiwan, Hong Kong, and other foreign countries?!

 That was a mystery to me, too, but their artwork is totally amazing! Perhaps they don't have so many places to showcase their artwork in their own countries. We warmly welcome art like this, but we'd also love to look at art from people like S here, who are just starting out.

 Yeah! I see pictures that are so awesome, and it makes me too nervous to do my navigating duties. I want to see lots of art from people who are beginners like me!

 Check out the how-to pages and the materials pages, and try them all out. And once your illustrations are complete, send them to *Style School*! We want to hear how you felt while creating the images and what problems you had, too!

 Then I'll get better, and then, hopefully, one day I'll get a job as an illustrator . . .

 Better believe it! We've also set up "Special Stage" pages for some of the people who sent us artwork, and we hope to have other kinds of work for contributors in the future as well.

 I see. By the way, has art in the 22nd century gotten more beautiful, like you'd expect?

 Well, what happens to illustration in the future, whether it becomes even more wonderful . . . that all begins with *you*, S, and the people who contribute to *Style School*!

 Wow . . .

 As everyone's art gets better and better, I will attain the objective of my quest through time! But to start with, you're going to have to do a lot of hard work, S!!

 With pleasure!

 Great! Well, S-"O" has used up all its power, so until next time!

 Till next time!

Check out the last page to learn how to contribute your illustrations to *Style School*! Your art may be published in *SS Magazine* in Japan!

STYLE SCHOOL vol. 1
エスエス

ILLUSTRATION AND INSTRUCTION

Cover illustration:
Yutaka Mizutani

Publisher
Mike Richardson

Editor
Chris Warner

Publication Design & Photography
Sasaki Yayoi

Design Assist
Heidi Fainza

Dark Horse Manga
A division of Dark Horse Comics, Inc.
10956 SE Main Street
Milwaukie OR 97222
darkhorse.com

First Edition: September 2007

ISBN-10: 1-59307-625-8
ISBN-13: 978-1-59307-625-2

art · Imperial Boy

art · Rio Nanami

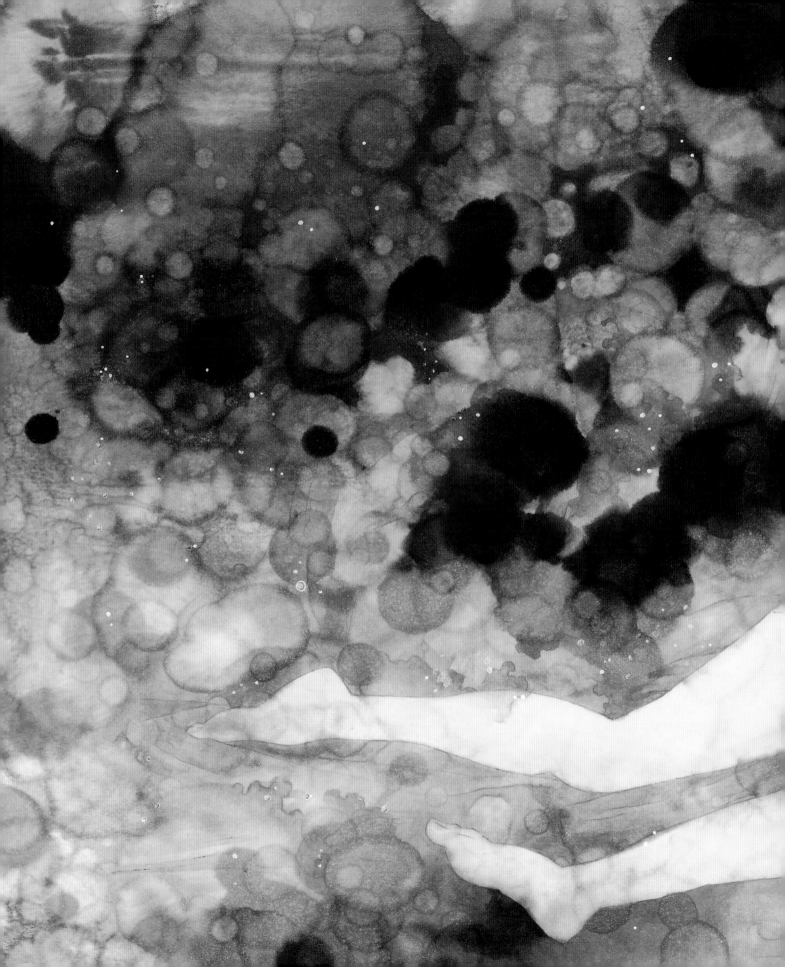

art · Dite

you who are heartless.....

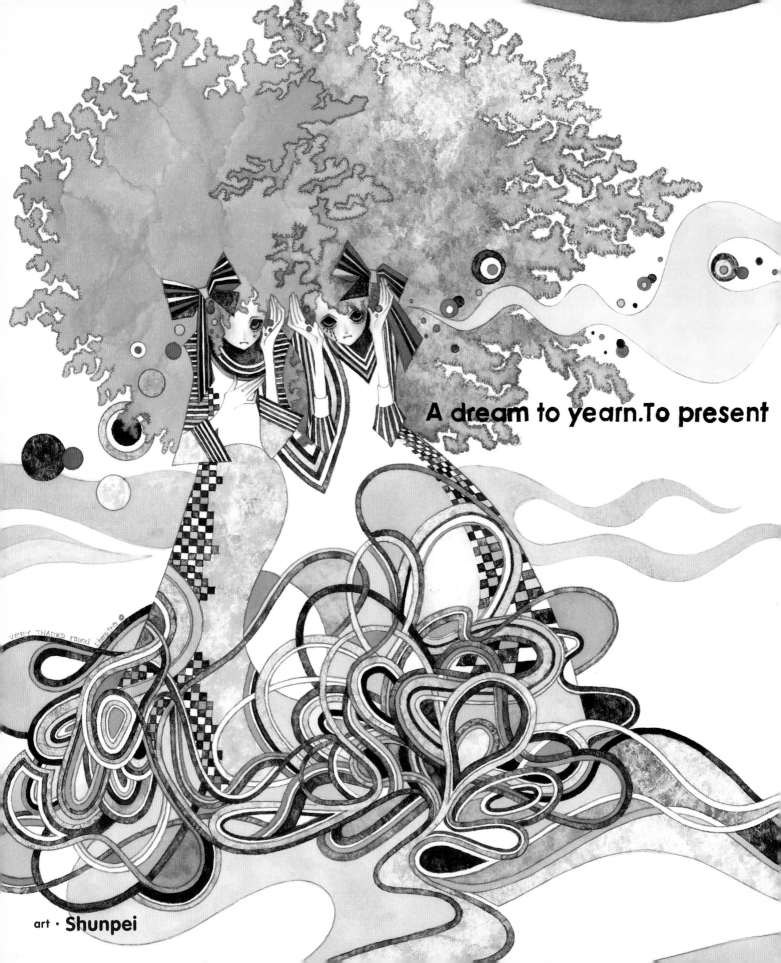

A dream to yearn.To present

art · Shunpei

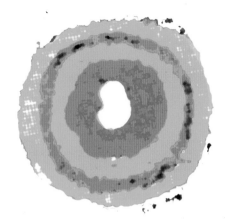

art · Miake

creating with markers

Babiry typically works with Copic markers. They're the ideal tools for doing light-hearted color illustrations. Even though easier to use than paints, the colors are just as vivid, and the selection of colors is abundant. The flesh-tone expression is powerful. Here we give you a breakdown of the process by which Babiry created this fantasy illustration of a boy and girl back-to-back. Babiry uses layers of color to create multicolored hues!

3 Use CM25 for deep skin tones in shadowed areas. Apply it to points like eyelids, spaces between tufts of hair, and parts of the nose.

2 Babiry uses CM14 for the base skin tone. Apply this color lightly over the whole area, except areas to be highlighted, which should be left white.

1 First, lay down a foundation of transparent "0." With this in place, colors added over it will become lighter.

fleshtones

A gradation of skin tones is created by carefully layering a base skin tone, deep skin tones, pink, etc.

6 Now again add CM14 to blend the pink with the skin tone. This is how gradations in the skin tones are created. Even if you use strong colors, adding lighter colors will blend them, and any unevenness due to color distinctions will disappear.

5 To add a pinkish red tint to the skin, add CM3 to the cheeks, just under the eyes. Because this is being added over the skin tone, the color will appear quite deep for the moment.

4 To blend the distinct light and dark areas from steps 2 and 3, use CM14 to give gradation to the edges of the colored areas.

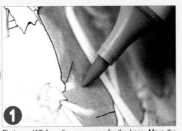

3 Add deep green G82 around the upper chest area. Because this area is under the arm, you want to create a sense of shadow in the hue.

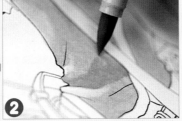

2 Once it dries, the color will lighten. Add BG32 around the waist. You'll get a brighter green than the base, creating a vivid impression.

1 First, use W3 from the gray group for the base. Move the brush smoothly down along the edges of the lines. While still wet, quickly add BG10 from the green group over the top. Layering the colors before they dry ensures that they'll mix well, and you'll get a deep green.

the girl's clothes

Here we create the colors and patterns in the girl's clothes using numerous colors, and also express the shadows and highlights.

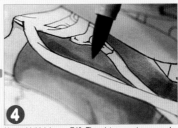

6 Where the shadows are stronger, use deep purple V06. The area where the fabric wrinkles and sticks out needs to be highlighted, so adding thick color above and below it will create a sense of solidity. Adding transparent #0 to the highlighted area will dissolve and lighten the color beneath it.

5 Use light purple BV000 to add bars to the top. We're not so much creating a pattern but an unevenness in the fabric which is shadowed to look like stripes. Blending in some light purple BV000 creates the foundation for this.

4 Now add thick brown E43. The mixture creates a complex color that adds depth to the image.

the girl's hair

Laying rich colors onto the base color of the hair creates a sense of volume and an impression of the hair's flow.

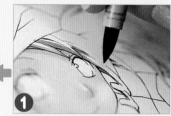

4 Add a layer of the reddish-brown E04. Cover everything from the top down, blending it with the base, to give the hair a slightly red tint.

3 Sweep the brush inwards, adding layers lightly. Because we intend to later add highlights, paint from each edge to the tips.

2 Use the same E71 to paint the hanging curl of hair. Add lots of color to the edges where the hair tapers and shadows would occur.

1 Use E71 from the brown group for the base. The bangs are sharp, so they should be painted with downward strokes. Since the shadow of the hair falls on the flesh tone beside it, paint it lightly with the same color.

7 Add another layer of brown E71, which was used for the base, to blend the colors and eliminate overly distinct colored areas and add unevenness to create a sense of volume.

6 Use E77 for the thick parts of the hair. There will be deep shadows on the bangs and the edge of the hairs sticking out at the side, so they need to be emphasized. Paint along the direction the hair is growing.

5 Add bright yellow Y00 in the areas that have been left white. These are the highlights. Add it to the borders of the brown areas as well, blending them and creating gradations to the different colors.

the girl's eyes

Layer and blend greens, and create a sparkle in the eye.

2 Add a tiny bit of yellow-green YG13 dead center for the pupil. We'll be creating a sense of the edge slowly blending away.

1 First, add transparent #0. As when coloring fleshtones, it will create more effective blending for subsequent colors.

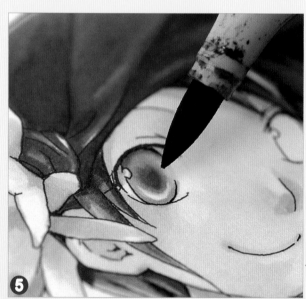

5 Finally, one last time, color the pupil with G7. The eye is all green, but it comes out a subtly graded layering of four colors. Because the eyes are wet, they reflect lots of light and are more complicated than other parts of the body. Layering similar colors creates the desired effect.

4 Add a thick bit of yellow-green G14 dead center, and then immediately blend in light green G40 at the boundary. The blurring effect creates the illusion of a pupil.

3 Use the same YG13 at the edge of the iris using the pen line as a guide to create a circular fringe.

the boy's hair

The boy's silver hair will gain the appearance of solidity simply by adding shadows.

1 Use the lightest of the light blues, BG000, to color any areas of the hair where shadows fall. The pen lines depict tufts of hair jutting out, and the shadows will fall under those tufts.

4 It would be kind of dull for the entire back of the head to have a uniform darkness to it, so we add highlights. You should still have some small unpainted areas. Create white in these areas with transparent 0. The gray will blend with the 0 and become white.

2 The spaces between tufts of hair will be darker. Color these areas with light purple BV000 to create the image of a sky blue turned almost black. Use a sweeping motion.

5 Finally, while keeping an eye on the overall balance, add watercolor BG000, and add light yellow-green G40 to the front edges of the hair to create highlights where light is reflected.

3 Layer the shadowed areas with C2 from the gray group, which will also strengthen the image of the silver hair. The back of the head will be in shadow, so color the entire area.

the completed picture

Babiry used several layers of colors to complete the picture. She started using this technique in junior high school, when she was painting a picture lit by moonlight. The clothing was purple, but she added yellow highlights to match the light of the moon and create the proper mood. The play of light is critical, because it creates the attractiveness and profundity of the picture. Because Copic comes in so many colors, it becomes even more tempting to try them all. And while it's fun trying out different colorful patterns in the clothing, it's even more interesting if you add in oranges and greens to create the effect of light. Creating a multihued image like this one is simple, even though no paints or mixing was needed. Now try out your own coloring techniques!

the boy's pants

The pants are mostly blue but include orange, pink, and green to colorfully represent reflected light.

5 Add in a deep navy blue BV23 at the top of the pants, and once it dries, add another layer of thick BV23 on top of it, giving it a rich finish.

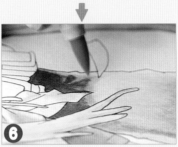

6 Add light green G40 to the area above the light orange and its border. We use varying colors to create areas where their distinctions can jump out vividly.

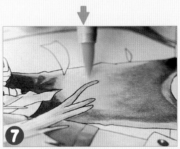

7 Add pink RV10 to the highlighted area. The color transitions are becoming more and more abundant. The pants are blue, but the pink group adds a different impression, creating bold highlights.

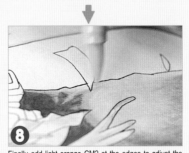

8 Finally add light orange CM2 at the edges to adjust the color tone. The edges are backlit, so we're creating the impression of light hitting them from the opposite side.

1 First, use light green G40 to color along the left edge, and use orange CM2 on the parts of the calves that jut out (which will be highlighted). Light hits the legs, so we want them bright.

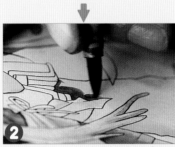

2 Start adding deep navy blue BV23 from the top. Because the cloth is hanging down and we don't want it to appear to stick out at any point, be careful to stick to the edge.

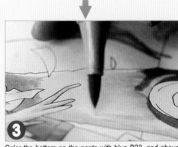

3 Color the bottom on the pants with blue B23, and above that brush in light purple BV000. The higher you get, the closer you'll be to the highlighted area, so keep the colors thick at the bottom and light higher up.

4 Now add light orange CM2, blending it in with the border of the light purple BV000 to create a bright area.

one point! "the pinky finger test"

During the coloring process, Babiry frequently checked colored areas against her pinky finger. This way she checks the differences between areas which have and haven't been colored for the overall balance, and to make sure colored areas have produced the right color tone.

artist **foo***
creating with Photoshop

working environment
OS: Windows XP
Memory: 512MB
HDD: 60GB+16GB
Scanner: Canon Multi PASS C50
Adobe Photoshop 5.5

foo* uses Photoshop for her illustrations. With a reddening sky in the background, the happy-looking girl on the roof with her fluttering hair creates a dramatic impression. In this section, we show all the tiny details that foo* put into the creation of this image, from the pen and ink drawing to the cats and the birdcage!

reading the line drawings into the computer

① Read the completed line drawings into the computer with a scanner set to grayscale and 400dpi.

② Under Image→Color Adjustment→Brightness/Contrast, increase the brightness and contrast to clear away any smudges from the line drawing, being careful not to eliminate or fade any fine lines. Use the brush tool to correct any overextended lines. Then, under Image→Resolution, drop the resolution to 350dpi, and under Image→Mode set the picture to RGB.

making the line drawings transparent

Select the entire image and Copy it. Then Paste it in Quick Mask Mode. At the bottom of the tool box are two buttons. When the one on the left is selected, you're in "Edit in Standard Mode"; pushing the right button will switch to "Quick Mask Mode."

foo*: "In Quick Mask Mode, selected areas will be white, unselected areas will appear red."

edit in standard mode

edit in quick mask mode

Because Example 3 is in Quick Mask Mode, the line drawing comes out red.

④ foo*: "Now, everything other than the line drawing is selected, so under the Select menu choose Inverse to make the line drawing itself selected."

⑤ Create a new layer, and cover the new layer in dark brown. Now if you erase the background layer (the original black & white line drawing we scanned in) the line drawing becomes transparent.

foo*: "If you make the line drawing transparent, it becomes easy to change the layer mode when the image is being composed. In the above illustration, the grayness comes from the white background being changed to transparent."

⑥ Once each of the three separate line drawings has been made transparent, move the three layers to a new file at original art size (and RGB, 350dpi), and adjust their position.

⑦ "Add Layer Mask" and erase any overlaps in the line drawing.

foo*: "If you add black on top of the layer mask, it clears away lines like an eraser; and if you use white erased parts come back, so even if you erase too much, it's easy to get back. I use the layer mask to adjust the bounds of each layer."

1. rough line drawing

First of all, in order to generally settle on the image, we need to create a color rough in Photoshop. Once the number of colors and their positions have been decided, they are used as a base to go from the rough line drawing to the actual line drawing.

overall flow

① foo* says of the feeling she went for, "We want to give the gusty roof, the peaceful wind, the flying object, and the birdcage shades of meaning . . . with yellow clouds in the greenish sky and points of orange."

② Using #1 above as a base, make a detailed rough sketch, fixing up the position of the motifs, sizes, and designs. Print out the corrected version in light blue on photocopying paper. Do the flying object, people, and cats on three separate sheets, then use a 0.3 or 0.5 mm mechanical pencil to trace directly over the lines.

foo*: "You can use this technique to create a line drawing even if you don't have a light box, and there's no need to erase the drawing underneath. Also, since you've still got the rough, you can go back to check your work against the initial image while you're working."

③ Putting together the pieces, we get the completed line drawing. The drawing of the roughs and making them transparent are all done through the clever use of Photoshop. Now we can move on to the stage of coloring this image.

2. rough coloring

After using the gradation tool to create the sky, you want to create new layers on which to add colors while comparing them to the original color rough. Then for each piece, you need to create "basic color layers" in which to add detailed separate colors.

sky

Set the general color tone using the gradation tool.
foo*: "It's difficult to create analog-like gradations in Photoshop. But since it's easy to work with graphics in Painter, I sometimes 'hand-paint' the gradations in Painter, adding different gradations for separate angles and forms."

background

The color tone of the clouds, the distant view, and the flying object are added on subsequent layers.
foo*: "Right now it's like we're setting up a standard against which the main characters will be colored in."

people and cats

Cover the skin, clothes, and hair with conspicuous colors using the pencil tool and in separate layers.
foo*: "Call these layers with separate colors basic color layers . . ."

foo*: "Next, I created a basic color layer for the flying object."

Once the basic color layers are complete, go to Image→Adjustments→Hue/Saturation to adjust them.

Check the "Lock Transparent Pixels" box in the basic color layers, and add in most of the shadows.

Use the eraser tool to clear any colors that cross lines.

---

cat's patterns

Only shadowed.

Create a "multiply" layer and place it over the cat's basic color layer. Select "Group with Previous" from the Layer menu, and you can add color without parts sticking out from the basic color layer intruding.
foo*: "I patterned the ears and face so it looked kind of like a Burman. I added white to the chest on a 'saturation' layer. I also added in the whiskers."

completed image

foo*: "I patterned each of the cats, the boy's clothes, and the girl's lace choker. I also added clouds."

---

4. coloring "patterns"

lace

foo*: "Don't try to illustrate the lace; illustrating the holes is much faster."

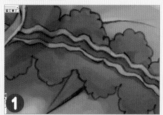

Group a "multiply" layer with the clothing basic color layer, and color in the lace parts.

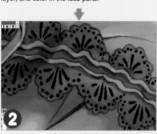

In a new "normal" layer, draw in the holes directly with black.

Check the "Lock Transparent Pixels" box, and use the Alt key to pick up the color of the cloth that will appear through the holes.

Add further "normal" layers above the line drawing layers to add highlights and make further adjustments.

Repeat the process of steps one through three to color in the clothing and hair.
foo*: "As I was finishing up, I lightened the color of the sky to express the open space, so now I colored the boy at the back to match the contrast."

Shadows on the people and cats are complete.

---

3. detailed coloring of people and cats

Here, using the brush and eyedropper tools, we further adjust the shadows added into the basic color layers created in Stage 2, "Rough Coloring," above.

Adjust the basic shadows with the brush tool while trying to stay conscious of the light source.

foo*: "You can press the Alt key with the eyedropper to pick up colors in the image; so you can pick up reflected colors and spread them out and adjust them with the brush tool."

5. detailed coloring of the background

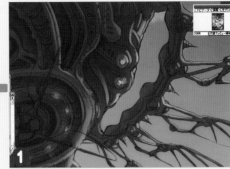

3 Because the birds are far away, we don't need to illustrate them in detail, but the nearest flock needs shadows added. Color the roof and the distant buildings and clouds basically the same.
foo*: "I think it's best to color the distant objects with dropped contrast. Because the line of the roof wasn't very clear, I drew the section in directly with the brush."

2 While fading the line drawing of the flying object, add gradation to it with layer masks to give it a sense of distance. Apply the gradations you created on the "normal" layer onto the color layers to give it an overall feel. Color in the wings on a new "screen" layer, and make the wingtips pink.

1 Add in shadows to the flying object as you did with the people.
foo*: "I added dim lights on a new 'dodge' layer."

6. the birdcage

5 Add shadows to the cage under the girl's hand, and adjust the lines around the cage, etc.

4 Unite the layers in which the birdcage was composed and position the cage. Adjust the placement, and change the color to golden. Using a Layer Mask, erase the parts where the girl's leg and hand overlap it. Add shadows where the cage sits over the girl's left leg and clothing.

3 Color the rear of the cage darker than the front, and lower the contrast.

2 Color the front of the cage.

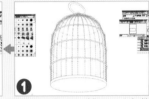

1 Putting together curved lines created with the Path Tool, with opposing lefts and rights, results in a birdcage shape.
foo*: "Because I wanted to give the cage its own weight, I created it separately from the line drawings, which will be in front and behind."

the completed picture

Brimming with liveliness and depth, this remarkable illustration is complete. With several separate layers, the addition of fine shadows, and color adjustments, vivid coloring brings this beautiful picture to life. Making the line drawings transparent and using layer masks are techniques that foo* often uses effectively in her work, and now you know why. They make for easy color adjustments and corrections, and you won't have to start from scratch if you make a mistake. Bearing these things in mind, even people who've never used Photoshop before can now try it out!

7. color adjusting

Here we adjust the overall color tone. Print out the picture from time to time to check the colors and contrast.

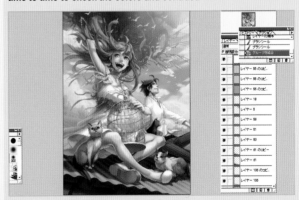

To create the lens-flare effect caused by the strong sunlight, you need to add on an "overlay" layer of orange and "screen" layer of golden yellow. Next, cover it with a "lighten" layer of blue-green. The "lighten" layer will look for darker colors than the ones in place and use only those colors to unify the colors of the dark areas of the whole picture.
foo*: "Because my colors always tend to be all over the place, this is the layer that saves me. (The 'darken' layer is the opposite: it uses only colors lighter than those already used. Both are helpful.) Finally, in an 'overlay' layer of golden yellow, I give the whole thing a yellow tint, and the front of the roof, which has very little color variation, gets 'dodged' in yellow. So finally I upped the contrast of the whole picture and dropped the saturation a bit."

The attractive nature of Yoshitsugi's illustration is in the beautiful blending of colors. The figure stands out in white, surrounded completely in a scene of numerous splashed hues. The vivid colors and impression of translucency are characteristic of the colored inks that were used in the creation of this image, which deeply stain paper soon after application. Mixing of these inks with water is common, but often the colors spread surprisingly more because of the water. Yoshitsugi used this effect in this piece, to create this dazzling image.

the basic process

The figure in the picture stands out in white, but to start with Yoshitsugi draws an outline of the figure in pencil. Then he erases it bit by bit and uses the faint lines left behind as guidelines for adding the colored inks. This is the basic process throughout. Because some areas will require bold blending and others will need light coloring, before coloring in light areas the ink needs to be sopped a bit with a tissue before applying it to the paper. If not, the ink will spread across the paper, and fine details won't be paintable.

  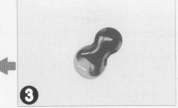 

4 Now to paint the skin. But before you do, wipe off the end of the brush with a tissue, leaving just a tiny bit of ink.

3 Drop some ink onto a piece of paper, which will serve instead of a palette. The colors here are vermillion and yellow.

2 Erase the pencil lines only of the area you're about to paint.

1 First, draw in the picture with pencil, creating the outlines of a line drawing.

flowers

The flowers are painted in thickly. Again, erase the line drawing as you add color. The colors used here are vermillion, yellow, cherry red, and sienna in the rich parts. The color changes according to the amount of water added, and you can use that light and dark variation to produce different kinds of flowers in their coloration. The pistils, etc. are drawn in with crayon. There are points where the flower petals will be solid and other parts graded, but the tips of the petals should be colored deeply, and the middle areas should be whiter, so adjust the colors here by blending them.

2 The parts being painted above are the petal tips, so they're painted thickly. The inner flower parts to the left will be blended in.

1 Erase the pencil lines only where you're going to paint at that moment. Work at it bit by bit.

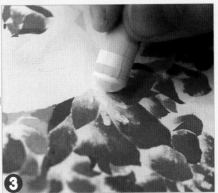

3 Once the color inks are dry, color added on top with crayon will cling to the inks.

4 This is the bird's head, but since the color is close to that of the flowers, we paint it at the same time.

the bird's feathers

The bird's feathers in the scenery also follow an initial pencil drawing, which is then erased as each bit is painted. As you can see from the photos below, you don't want to erase the lines completely. Because these will be a guide for coloring, we need to leave faint outlines behind as a kind of target. After applying the colored inks, the pencil lines will all be erased cleanly. Sienna and yellow were used for the feather colors. After adding the color, stretch it out with a water brush to give it light gradations.

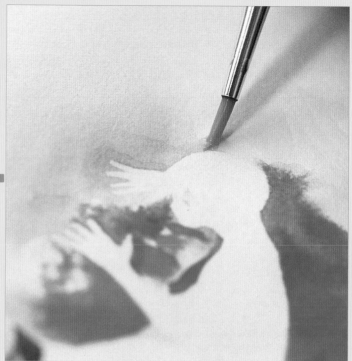

the scenery over the figure's head

This is where the characteristic coloring-by-blending style of Yoshitsugi's image really begins. First, at the top of the figure's head, begin by adding lots of water to your brush, and spread the water out where you intend to color. This creates a mask-like effect, and where water has been added the colored inks will follow suit, spreading their color. By doing this, none of the inks will leak onto the figure's head. While the paper is wet, you only need to just touch the paper with your brush and the colors will spread in an instant. Use this trick to create blotches in several areas, using you brush to mix blotted areas into each other where desired.

the image after drying

After some time has passed and the colors have dried, the image will look like this. The figure stands out in white well enough, but we can see some of the blotch variations too clearly. Also, there are parts that are deeply blurred, and parts that are lightly blurred, so above the character's head, as you can see in the photo, the red is there but it's too light. This is because we tried to control the volume of the ink after it was on the paper. Because we used inks with lots of water on the paper, if you run your brush over it before it dries, places that are heavily colored can be adjusted. However, this problem can't be corrected after drying, so it's necessary to be aware of this from the beginning of the coloring process.

The background is quite rich, so we're coloring it with sienna-added vermillion. Looking at the photo, you can see the ink is very damp with water. Use lots of water as we've done here, and be bold when adding your color to get the best blurring.

If you add ink over the crayon, the oil-based crayon lines will repel the water and jump out in bold relief. An impressive contrast is created between the crayon white and light red of the color inks. Looking at the lower photo, by thickly adding more colors, both the strongly colored parts and the white crayon stand out, creating interesting nuances. Complete the scene in this fashion.

Once the colors have been somewhat set in place, use a water brush to spread the inks and move the colors just a tiny bit. You can create light blotching this way, too. It's okay to use a brush with a tiny bit of color already in it. In this case, use a tissue to pick up some of the dampness off of the brush before starting. By creating light blurred areas beside the deep blurred ones, the color transitions in the overall image will come out quite beautiful.

the complete picture

This is the complete image with the motifs of the bird's tail taking up much of the space, and the child beside it. The scene is beautiful, being completely blotched in red. The bold use of inks to create vivid coloring characteristically brings to life the expression of the blotching, and the combination of colors also greatly affects one's impressions. If you find it interesting, you should try it out at least once!

brushes

Yoshitsugi uses thick brushes to create the bold blurring in the scenery, and extra-fine brushes for lightly painting detailed areas.

colored inks

Yoshitsugi uses Holbein drawing inks and Sakura crayons. Both are basic art materials that can be bought inexpensively. Peeking out from behind the eraser is a peanut, which guards the artist.

artist **Noa**

creating with watercolors

Noa paints with transparent watercolors. As the name suggests, their unique characteristic is their transparency, and any other colors or the paper beneath them show through. What makes them different from non-transparent watercolors (gouache) and acrylic paints is that with those paints, adding more layers covers the colors underneath. The beauty of transparent watercolors comes from gradations created by layers, and they exhibit excellent results when you want to create ethereal moods. Because Noa wanted to create a picture with pale color transitions and wanted the natural color of the paper to show through, watercolors were the perfect choice.

masking

The very first step is to create protective "masks" in areas the colors can't be allowed to run into. Use frisket as you would with any other paints to cover the area you want to mask. It will come out looking blackish, but because it is resin-like, colors will not run into these areas and they will remain white. Once the paint dries, the frisket can be stretched and peeled off, and when peeled off in the final stages, places that haven't been colored will be revealed. In this case, the window frame, leaves on the tree, and the birdcage were masked.

Noa's brushes

Noa uses everything from mid-sized to extra-fine brushes. You can see the range in the picture above, which compares them with a pencil.

painting the background

4 Looking at the distinctions between neighboring colors, you can see how the blue and green have mixed. Create color transitions in this manner.

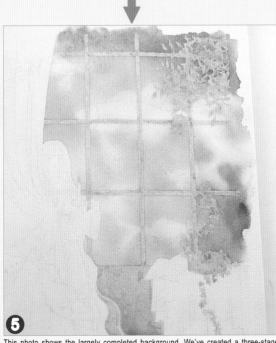

5 This photo shows the largely completed background. We've created a three-stage gradation of colors from yellow to green to blue. Because we want the floating fish to appear phantasmal, we've left them vaguely unpainted to later give them a sense of being lightly colored.

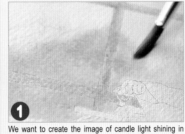

1 We want to create the image of candle light shining in the night, so first paint the candle light in Permanent Yellow Deep.

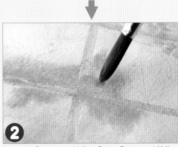

2 Next mix Permanent Yellow Deep, Permanent Yellow Orange, and Gamboge Nova to get a green, and paint it outside the candle light.

3 Now we need to add a blue outside to represent the night. This is a mix of Sepia, Burnt Amber, Royal Blue, Cobalt Blue Hue, Blue-Gray, and Horizon Blue.

spread water over parts to be painted

Spread water over the places you're going to add color. Doing this will make it less likely for the colors to slowly spread unevenly to other parts of the paper when these areas are painted.

Because we don't want paint to run into areas we plan to leave unpainted, add water even to tiny areas with a fine brush. Because we're working on the background, we don't want paint to run onto the figure.

hair

Start with a pale undercoat, finally adding lines of shadow.

4 Finally, to complete the image add fine lines like these for shadows, and yellow lines the same color as the candle light to show their reflection.

3 Paint other locations lightly in the same way. Think about it in the same way you applied water in the beginning.

2 Paint the hair drooping down over her torso. Be careful not to cross the lines of the line drawing.

1 Start painting the hair from the peak of the head. Because light is coming from the candle in the girl's hand, the top of the head will be darker.

clothing

Add color only to the shadowed areas so the clothes themselves appear white.

3 This is what it looks like when the base shadows have been added. As the entire image approaches completion and you get a sense of the overall feel, you can add more layers to the shadows bit by bit to make them darker.

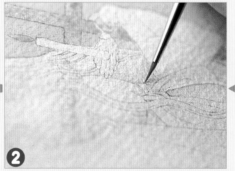

2 Carefully do the folds in the fabric and the cloth around the waist in the same way. The highlights will be the unpainted areas where the paper white shows through.

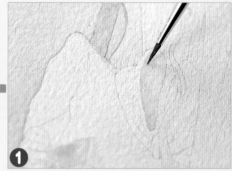

1 First, paint the inside of the ribbon hanging from the girl's waist, which will have very dark shadows. Work delicately with an extra-fine brush to create a dark to light gradation from the edge.

One Point!
transparent fish

You can see clear through the floating fish. From the beginning, we never gave these a clear outline and just left unpainted vague forms where they'd be. Paint the fish lightly with the same colors used for the background (which you would see transparently behind the fish), and paint the protruding highlighted parts of the fish white. This will give the fish a sense of three-dimensionality while at the same time creating the impression of their transparency. If you add water again before the paint dries to lighten the color, it will create a faint blending effect. Then add white to blend it closer to the background color. Repeating this will produce a delicate sense of transparency.

eyes

Layer the colors bit by bit to create the depth of the eyes.

With the eyes, as before, color the irises very lightly, as you did with water at first, making them darker in coats. The whites of the eyes and highlights will remain unpainted, so use an extra-fine brush to paint only the necessary areas bit by bit. In the case of this illustration, the tops of the eyes are dark and the lowers parts are highlighted, so we thickly coat the upper parts of the irises.

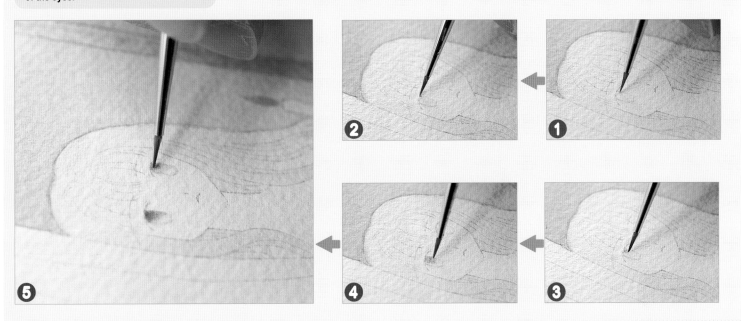

the completed picture

The result is gradations of color from the candle light and transparent floating fishes. Transparent watercolors are perfect for this kind of painting, which emphasizes the beauty of blended and overlapped colors. The patterns on the curtain were painted in piece by piece, using the technique of layering after drying, using an extra-fine brush to create a pale finish. The resulting beautiful effect creates a distinct world.

One Point!
removing the masking

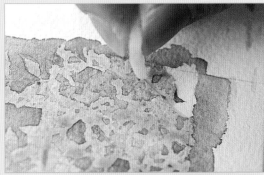

When removing the masking it will peel off gum-like, like dried glue. Lightly rubbing it will cause the masking substance to peel off slowly, and the white surface will appear. After pulling off the masking from the completed picture, the spaces were then painted, but this is also a useful tool if you want to just leave something pure white.

artist Satono Sakiyama

creating with acrylics

Satono Sakiyama uses Liquitex acrylic paints. These paints are useful because they can be lightened with water to make them paler like watercolors, or they can be used thick, as-is, like oil paints for heavy colors. They dry quickly, so adding layers of color doesn't cause them to mix but just leaves the new color on top. The ability to use various layering techniques makes them convenient for Satono. Now, Satono shows us how to paint lightly with acrylics!

the boy's face

First, color the dark parts of the skin, then use a water brush to spread those colors to other areas.

The color used here was a mixture of Dioxazine Purple, Titanium White, Pure Red, and Burnt Sienna. Since this entire image has a blue cast, we used purple-ish paint to get blueness in the skin.

   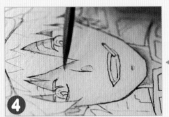

④ Complete the rest of the face in this way, using water to spread the color and create gradations.

③ Fill your brush with even more water, and draw the color inwards from the edge of the cheeks.

② Paint the cheeks, using more water in your brush than you did before.

① First add thick skin tone in the shadow of the hair and the shadow of the chin.

the boy's hair

Bearing the overall picture in mind, we create a color to match the purple and pink tone of the rest of the picture.

The hair color is made with the same colors used for the background: Ultramarine Blue and Dioxazine Purple with added Mars Black.

② Add thick paint to the very top part of the head. Create gradations by spreading the paint down to the lighter areas.

① First, paint the rearmost hair by the neck with a thick, solid coat. After that, use the same color mixed with water to do the top of the head.

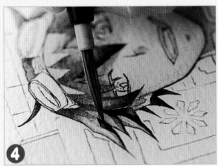 

④ Since the mountain-shaped areas are highlighted, add pink to them. Since all of the bright areas in the overall picture contain pink, we do the same here in consideration of that balance.

③ Rotate the paper to a position that's easier to paint in to do the front hairs. Again, spread the paint to make it lighter, but since we're going to paint the mountain-shaped parts of the hair a different color, leave them clean.

One Point!
how to add lots of water

After adding water to her brush, Satono wipes off some of the excess with a tissue before painting. Then she uses a tissue to pick up some of the dampness from the painted areas. When using water to thin the paints, the proper quantity is critical. Adding too much could totally fade the color, and too much running is also unacceptable, so water needs to be added bit by bit in each instance through painstaking repetitions to complete the lightly painted areas.

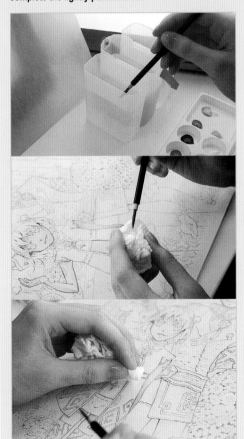

033

the boy's eyes

Layer vivid colors over the center of the eyes, and blend with gradations.

① Use the Ultramarine Blue and Dioxazine Purple to distinctly paint the eyelashes.

② Next, paint the brims of the irises with the same color, and add solid, thick paint to their centers.

③ Use water to draw color from the top lashes downward. Use a tissue to wipe up excess from the whites of the eyes to prevent them from being over-painted.

⑥ We're adding layers, yellow over green and purple in the middle of the eye, so complete the job by working in light gradations.

⑤ For the bottom of the iris, use the strong yellow Yellow Medium Azo. This will give an accent to the eyes.

④ Paint the iris. Start with Ultramarine Blue, then add Turquoise Green to Dioxazine Purple and start painting from the top of the iris.

the chest crest

Use a fine brush with almost no water to paint in distinct colors.

Finely patterned details are easy to paint in when using Liquitex. Use the line drawing as a guide for adding color. We want the colors of the outside triangles to stand out, so paint them in solidly. The leaf pattern inside the circle will be lighter, so paint one portion of it thickly, and then spread that paint to the other areas to thin it out. The key is to only use a tiny bit of water so the colors don't run. Finally, paint in the light spots in the middle of the pattern with white. Because Liquitex colors don't mix when layered, it's easy to just add more coats after drying.

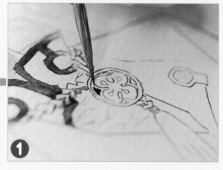

①

②

③

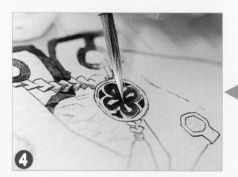

④

the boy's clothing

First, paint in the shadows, then paint in the rest of the clothing to match that color tone.

3 Fill your brush with water to spread out the colors you painted into the shadows before. Acrylic dries quickly, so even using water over it won't blotch or ruin the areas you've already painted.

1 Create a color mix of Ultramarine Blue, Dioxazine Purple, and Mars Black, and paint the sides first.

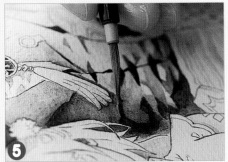

5 To add deep colors to the areas of darkest shadow, keep adding water-thinned paint and slowly stretch the colors out.

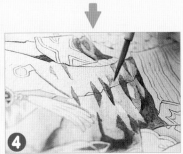

4 Use this technique to cover the entire area with a faint coat, to create a basic hue for the clothing.

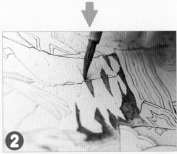

2 Next, move on to the folds in the middle of the jacket where shadows would appear, and paint them in.

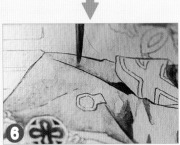

6 In places where very little shadow would occur, just use water to spread the existing color out, and complete coloring of all the clothing.

the completed picture

Completing the girl in the same way produces the final image. Satono's technique was to use lightly painted acrylic colors to create a base and to add thick, fixed colors with very little water in finely detailed areas. For the light areas, it's necessary to diligently and repeatedly add water to your brush, adding coat after coat, while also removing any excess water along the way. But the result of this thoroughness will be a delicate image. Acrylics are the ideal painting materials for those who do finely detailed line drawings, so be sure to try them out.

One Point!
color roughs

When creating this image, Satono created several color roughs. Looking at these, we can see what kinds of moods different color bases would have created. Color roughs can be helpful before you actually start coloring.

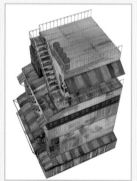

an example of 3D modeling

When deciding on a solid composition, the best point of view is reached by creating your building, or whatever it may be, in 3D and adjusting the angles. The 3D image is quite convenient because, like a real model, once it's created it can be turned around and viewed from all sides. You can even specify which side you want shadows to fall on, and they will be accurately produced. When dealing with things like buildings, which demand accuracy, 3D modeling software is the ideal tool.

artist

Imperial Boy

creating with 3D & 2D software

To create the illustration in our opening spread, Imperial Boy used the software LightWave 3D 6.5 for 3D work, and Photoshop 5.5 for 2D. He uses a homemade AT compatible computer with about 720 MB of memory. Before working with Photoshop, he precisely put all the elements of the scene together in 3D, even though most of the parts are not visible in the final completed image, and here's a look at the amazing process!

3D modeling

Here we'll explain the 3D model that was created for this picture. First we place the characters. It might help to think of these as mannequins on your computer. Here you can decide on the directions the characters are facing and their poses. The closer characters are bigger; the further characters smaller according to perspective. In this manner the characters can be placed to balance the image. Other functions, like adding shadows wherever characters are placed, can be executed automatically. Rendering the model in LightWave this way results in an image that can be opened in Photoshop. After importing it to Photoshop, use this model image to trace a rough over, and add details.

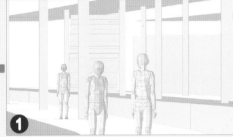

3 Fix the people's poses and change the colors so the scenery is easier to make out.

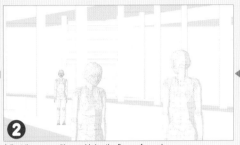

2 Adjust the composition and bring the figures forward.

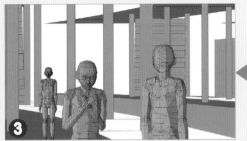

1 First, place the people on the train platform.

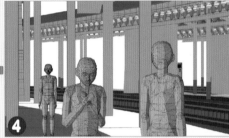

6 Draw a rough based on the model. Adding white makes drawing easy.

5 Place the people in the background.

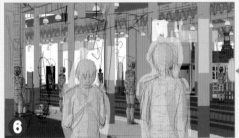

4 Detail the background of the platform.

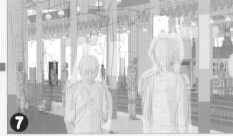

8 Start adding the rough details.

7 Cover everything in white. This will make creating the line drawing easier.

3D parts

Imperial Boy places images he created in 3D in the background, building the overall picture out of composite elements. They seem like they could have been recycled from other projects, but for the most part he creates new elements for each picture. As in the model of the platform that appears above, constructing a succession of parts to act as elements of the picture is a useful application of 3D modeling.

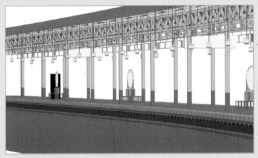

adding signs

adding light

the signs on the rear platform

Here we create the signs hanging down from the top of the rear platform. These are created separately and then pasted in. All parts with writing on them were created separately in Photoshop like this. Imperial Boy has created a unique script for this fictitious world. Because it's a sign that's meant to be lit by tube lights, add two bright highlight lines to the top and bottom.

the part

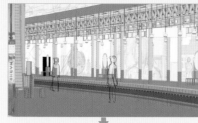

the rear platform

To complete the background, first remove the people. Make the rearmost platform out of 3D parts, as shown on the previous page. Create seats for the platform etc. out of 3D parts as well and position them, then add color in Photoshop. First, roughly start adding the significant colors by coloring the posts with yellow and green, which will be the base colors.

electric cables, advertisements, and signal over the platform

Add in the running cables, and the advertisements in the same way you did the signs above, and draw in the signal. Draw the signal as you would normally. Create a line drawing, then color it a single color, then finally color in the details. Imperial Boy worked on the line drawing, single color, and detailed color in three separate layers.

signal— line drawing

electric cables

signal— colored In

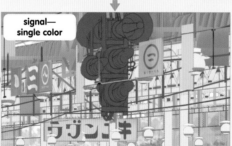

signal— single color

advertisements

pasting on signs

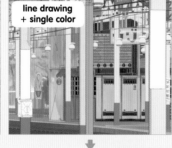

line drawing + single color

lighting

detailing

the front posts

Position and color the posts on the front platform the same way you did the ones at the back. Add a solid single color, then dirty it up. Next, add the warning signs, station name, advertisements, etc. Also add in the light striking them. This platform is covered, so from this camera angle the closest post will be darkened by shadow. Because the light's coming from across, the bottoms of the posts, which are not protected by the roof, will be brightly lit.

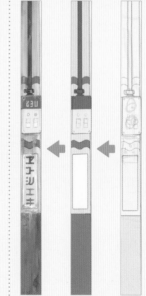

pole at the left edge

Draw in the left hand post on the front platform in three layers: line drawing, single color, and detail. Because this station's posts are meant to look old, after adding the single color, you want to give it a "dirty" look. Add the single color cleanly, but then use the multiply function to add brown and grey in random spots and create the appearance of dust, dirt, and soot.

small shop on the rear platform

single color (2)

add a mask (1)

To make the small shop on the rear platform, we first mask the area where the shop will be. The vending machines beside it are a 3D object created for a previous illustration and appropriated into this one. First, decide on the overall shape of the shop then give it an antiquated brown color. After that, add the sign with the writing on it. This is the train timetable. The lettering here doesn't mean anything, just a mix of numbers, Japanese, and English letters. Finally, we need to light it the way a train timetable would be, so we add bright bars across it as highlights to represent the light and dark bands of fluorescent lighting.

lighting (4)

add detail (3)

lighting the scene

Light hits the surface of the platform. We wanted to create the effect of the light filtering down, and even, gentle coloring will create a burst of spreading light. To give the environs of the rear platform a sense of dimension, add a light blue-grey over them at 25% transparency. Add brown to the sunlight at the front in the same way.

add shadows (3)

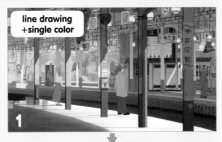

line drawing +single color (1)

lighting (4)

detailing (2)

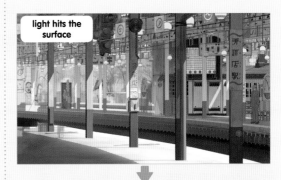

light hits the surface

the completed scenery (5)

This is the completed scenery. The scene itself has an extremely evocative mood. After this we'll add the main characters.

figures in the scenery

The people waiting for trains in the background are also drawn in three layers: line drawing, single color, and detailing. Distant figures don't need to be detailed any more than is necessary. In fact, to set the scene it's more important to invest energy into the effect of the lighting. Therefore, we add shadows and fade the color, and show light hitting the people's edges kind of like the image of light filtering through. This creates the sense of backlighting.

backlighting

drawing the main characters

Make everything white so it's easy to put in the line drawing, then detail in the rough drawing of the main characters. Complete the line drawing on a separate layer using the rough as a guide.

base colors for the figures

Once the line drawing is finished cleanly, add solid base colors and separate each area of color, creating layers of similar color for body parts like the skin and hair.

② Use Multiply to roughly color the hair. It doesn't matter if it goes over the lines.

① Make the clothes cream-colored, and use Multiply to make the lines transparent before coloring.

⑤ Add shadows and highlights to their hair.

④ Color the ribbon, skirt, bag, and other small parts.

③ Now color the skin. The girl's is whiteish. Color it a uniform, solid base color.

completing the figures

Since the girl's face is plainly visible, it needs to be colored in detail. We add shadows to the skin and make adjustments throughout. At this stage, because the eyes weren't exactly right, they were erased and redone.

③ The eyes are colored to create the expression.

② The red of the cheeks and other fine details are put in.

① The first stage of shadows in the girl's skin is added.

⑥ Finally, shadows are added to the clothing as well, and everything is fine-tuned.

⑤ The eyelashes of the redrawn eyes come out at the sides for completion.

④ At this stage, a more emotional expression was desired, so the eyes were redone.

composing figures with the background

Here we add figures over the completed background. The cheering girls were created relatively simply then added in. The letters on the sign were then added, then shadows, then all were darkened. And to add the shadow of the post, the post to be placed in front of the girls is copied from the background and the layer placed in front of them.

adjusting the color balance

Once the background and characters are combined, finally the colors have to be adjusted, so we try out several different color balances such as strongly bold contrast, greenish shadows, or full of orange light. Try out several patterns until you find a lighting you're happy with.

composition with the main characters

Read the completed image of the main boy and girl into the background scene. With Photoshop's Layer function, a picture that was created on a same-sized canvas will be placed in the same position, so work done in parts like this fits together smoothly.

the completed picture

And so the picture is complete: a scene of a girl confessing her crush to a boy on a station platform. Looking back over the whole process, and things like the rear platform and the train there, and all the parts that aren't actually seen in this image but were painstakingly created nonetheless, the final composition is incredibly complicated. At first glance, 3D modeling may seem like an overly mechanical way to work, but if you think of it like using miniatures or dolls for poses to make rough sketches, it is effective for creating accurate art. Imperial Boy himself makes a rough line drawing over the 3D so that it doesn't come off cold, and even though he used line tools in the background, he drew things at the front by hand. One straight line would lack nuance, so to give the picture warmth, create lines of varying thicknesses. The warmth in the picture comes from drawing the delicately shaky-lined people into the accurate picture.

transparent watercolors

colored inks

the right materials for you?

testing out color art supplies!

picture **Fumika**

Transparent watercolors produce a clear, lightly colored image. You can see the paper and other colors that are under the top coat. As you can see in the skirt in Fumika's picture, the characteristic blended unevenness of the skirt gives the image personality. Illustrators Zwerger, Yasuhiro Nakura, and Hiroyuki Asada use them. In the opening how-to pages, Noa used them. They produce beautiful results if you are placing emphasis on color transitions and pale colors.

Fumika: "I heard watercolors get prettier as you layer them, so I kept layering different colors on top of each other, but the lower coats dissolved and the end result was not what I expected. Also, the paper got conspicuously bumpy. But of course, there are instances when these things would be desirable. With acrylics, once they've dried on your palette you can't use them anymore, so if they dry while you're painting and you later think "I want to use that color I used before," you've got to mix it again, but you often don't get a perfect match. But with transparent watercolors, even if they dry, you just add water and the paint melts and you can use it again. I think that's really good. (Also meaning you can use your paints right up until they run out. I've thrown out a considerable volume of acrylics because they hardened on the palette before I got a chance to put them on paper. It's a huge waste.)"

Fumika used colored inks frequently in the past. In this issue's opening how-to pages, it was Yoshitsugi who used them. Colored inks are characterized by their transparency and vividness. Manga artists often use them. The clear and beautiful colors of manga artists Reiko Shimizu, Kaori Yuki, Kaoru Fujiwara, and Kosuke Fujishima are colored inks. Shou Tajima's technique is to use very light colors by adding a great deal of water to impressive effect. If you use water well, you can create a range of light to vivid images.

Fumika: "Overall, I like using colored inks best. While I'm painting and when the work is finished, I think it has a unique feel. I guess you could say it doesn't feel heavy . . . I've been using acrylics recently because inks fade easily, but if that wasn't the case I'd be using them. (I already had some that had turned brown in the jar, so I'm using it as brown. Someone gave it to me half-used, so I have no idea how old it is . . .) Also, one of the things that make inks difficult to work with is that if the color comes out uneven, you can't fix it. I've heard that it's better not to layer water-soluble colored inks, so first, other than the areas where I added light shadows, I created all the colors on my palette and applied them to the image in one go. I used masking tape to leave the stripes on the skirt white."

If you decide to work in color, there are so many kinds of materials to choose from, each producing different results. The colors come out differently, and you may end up with anything from a matte-like finish to a light transparency. Many people first choose their materials based on what the artists they admire use, but to reproduce the image in your head well, the properties of the materials themselves are very important. In this article, Fumika went through seven different types of art materials. We got her thoughts on each so you can learn about their unique characteristics, too!

acrylics

colored pencils

markers

Just add a little water, and acrylics are ready for thick applications and realistic detailing. When mixed with a lot of water, like watercolors they can be used for light blending effects. They dry quickly and are waterproof, and so once dry they can be painted over to make alterations or corrections. They also have a high transparency and leave a characteristic vivid, clear impression. In our opening how-to pages Satono Sakiyama used a soft technique for smooth, light coloring. Akemi Takada, Katsuhiro Otomo, Nobuteru Yuuki, and Yuuichi Kumakura are just a few artists who use acrylics.

Fumika: (Light coloring:) "Acrylics don't fade easily, and they dry waterproof, which made them easy to work with. With water-soluble paints, if you try to paint over something, you re-wet the colors underneath and they mix together, so if you make a mistake, it's not easy to fix. Another advantage of acrylics is that if you accidentally drip water on the painting, it won't leave any traces. And if you're not quite at the lines in some colored areas or there's unevenness, you can just add another layer to fix the problem. I use tape to mask, but when lightly coloring with acrylics, I've discovered they bleed, so I've switched to inks.

(Thick application:) "I put a really thick coat on the flower in this picture. You can use acrylics for fine detailing and use them like oils to paint on rough surfaces. Acrylics are easy to use compared to oil paints: they're odorless, and you can apply them with the same tools you use for watercolors. However, while you can make changes as many times as you like, this can cover the line drawing, and the mixed colors on your palette can dry out quickly, which is a headache."

Colored pencils make fine and delicate gradations possible. Since pencils are a tool most people are used to using, this is an easy medium to work with. The colors don't come out vividly, but since they can create fine color transitions, they're ideal for real representations of light and dark. The highest-quality colored pencils are those with no powdery-ness and a high oil content, which produce thick, dampish colors. They can also be used in combination with markers or acrylics, and many artists use their remarkable light and dark differentiation to give solidity to their works. Junko Kitano uses watercolor pencils, and Kouji Yamamura uses colored pencils in his animation.

Fumika: "I used to think you couldn't use colored pencils to create actual art, but then I realized I was thinking this way based on the colored pencils I'd used back in elementary school. The ones created specifically for this kind of art are easy to work with. I started coloring very thickly and was surprised how amazingly easy it was to layer. In the how-to books, the selling points of these specialized colored pencils seems to be that they can be applied thickly and their oiliness . . . and when I used them this seemed to be true. When coloring lightly, I'm not very good at pastel colors; I didn't know quite how to use them, and they came out too delicate. But still when compared to regular colored pencils, I think they were really easy to work with. Again, there are no smudges around the picture, you can use them anywhere easily, and they're easy to work with. Also, you don't have to rush to finish because you're worried about the colors becoming uneven as they dry. And if you're working very lightly, you can even clean up some of your mistakes with an eraser, which makes me very happy."

The standard materials for many manga artists in their work. They're convenient because they can be used right away without having to mix or dissolve paints. Because they're often used in manga illustration, there's an abundant selection of colors like flesh tones ideal for depicting characters. Ei-ichiro Oda, Takeshi Obata, and CLAMP all use them. In our how-to section, Babiry used them and the colors came out beautifully. Fumika used them in this picture, and the skin complexion came out nicely.

Fumika: "I did this on drawing paper, so the colors really blended. I feel like my pictures don't communicate well enough when using markers. It's more like, 'Was this done by a human?' It's even more conspicuous when the lines are clean and there don't seem to be any finger marks.

With markers, you don't have to worry about paint accidentally flying off your brush and splatting down somewhere, you don't have to clean any brushes, and there's no inadvertent getting paint on your hands and smudging it all over the place. It's great they're so easy to work with. That's why in the past when I was at events and drawing in sketchbooks, I used markers. I think their weak point is that to a certain degree they might not come in as many colors as you want and you sometimes can't produce the exact image you're envisioning."

materials used in this article

Colored Inks
(Dr. Ph. Martin's)
Watercolor Inks
Radiant Colors

Transparent Watercolors
(Holbein)
Holbein Transparent
Watercolors

Copic (Too)
Copic Sketch 36 Colors
Copic Chao 36 Colors

Colored Pencils
(Holbein)
Holbein Artist
Colored Pencils

Liquitex
(Bonny)
Acrylic Paints
(REGULAR)

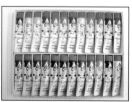

Acryla Gouache
(Holbein)
Holbein Acryla Gouache

Poster Colors
(Designers Colour)
Poster Colors
(Nicker Designers
Colour)

poster colors

Poster colors use the same pigments as nontransparent watercolors, and present bold colors. In order to avoid unevenness, they're often used for images that have clearly distinct color areas in their design. They're overwhelmingly used in animation, and the profound, realistic pictures that make up the animation backgrounds of which Japan is so proud are always done with poster colors. The strength of CG is in its lack of unevenness but poster colors are still in common use today because of their unique warmth and vividness.

Fumika: "My mother says in design offices these days they use the bucket tool for what they used to do with poster colors in the old days. But I think when using them for illustration, they have a different feel than what comes out of a computer. (Kind of like in animation, the difference between cell and computer colored animation?)

"These were easy to make corrections with, because once they dried you could just layer over them, but if you put on too many layers it seems like it started to crack. The line drawing disappeared, but when my mother drew over the paints with a pen, the powder got in the pen and stopped it up, and then she had to redraw out the lines with a brush. The water content is higher than acrylics and they're less sticky, creating a matte-like finish."

acrylic gouache

These are acrylic paints like Liquitex, but gouache is like nontransparent watercolor in its matte-like finish. Fumika used thick coats in parts of the hat. Gouache is inexpensive and easy to use. It dries quickly, and once dry is waterproof, so it too can be painted over. Its drying speed is fast compared to regular acrylics. Illustrator Komako Sakai uses them, and Kunihiko Tanaka used them back when he was still working by hand.

Fumika: "I wasn't sure exactly how to use the paints at first, because they were softer than I was expecting, but Sukemaru Ichita gave me a lesson and that improved it a bit. Because they're waterproof, I kept painting over previous layers without hesitation. Paints are handy that you can keep layering while slowly fine-tuning their color tones and delicately shifting the position of the shadows. It was fun getting that scratchy feeling in the brush, too. But when I added thick coats, the line drawing got wiped out, which caused some trouble. I also didn't like that they ran out so quickly (I'm super cheap)."

sky SCHOOL

color illustration collection

Thank you for sending us so many submissions for our very first issue!
Here we present everyone's lovely color illustrations!!

UKI • HOKKAIDO • AGE 25

EVAN・TAIWAN

TORU TAKURA • KANAGAWA

SWAY

HAL • NAGASAKI

AK • TAIWAN • AGE 22

ARIAKE • OKAYAMA • AGE 17

MITSUIRO • TOKYO • AGE 22

HAIJI • MIYAGI

914 KANA • FUKUOKA • AGE 19

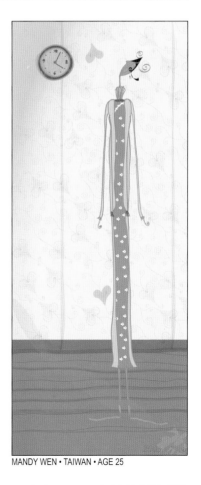

MANDY WEN • TAIWAN • AGE 25

COMAX • TAIWAN • AGE 31

SENZOKU KANEDA • OSAKA

JACK MONKEY

HACHI AYABE • SAITAMA

AO • TOKYO

SAIMAKI • KANAGAWA • AGE 27

MENBEI • IBARAGI • AGE 22

CHIZURU UNNO • TOKYO • AGE 20

ASUA SAEMURA • OSAKA

TAZU • NAGANO • AGE 25

AKIRA KIGAMI • OITA • AGE 21

NAGISAKO • SAITAMA • AGE 28

MOTSU • SAITAMA • AGE 17

SHINNO • FUKUOKA • AGE 38

CHEUNG NGA? • TAIWAN • AGE 25

KIKU TAKADA • OSAKA • AGE 25

SOUGYO MIZUGAME • TAIWAN • AGE 26

SORA • OSAKA • AGE 21

YOKUSA AGENDA • KYOTO • AGE 20

ACAI • TAIWAN • AGE 27

HITOE • CHIBA • AGE 17

PICOT • KANAGAWA • AGE 20

ANITA • TOKYO • AGE 14

SHIMADA • CHIBA • AGE 21

HINATA • TOKYO • AGE 33

ICHI • IWATE • AGE 14

TOBARI • OKAYAMA • AGE 20

SAKU TOMA • SAITAMA • AGE 28

AZUMI HIROSE • TOKYO • AGE 20

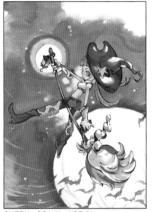

CHEBU • OSAKA • AGE 21

TAO YUUJI • AICHI • AGE 23

OKATI • FUKUOKA • AGE 24

WAKABA • FUKUOKA • AGE 20

YOSHIFUSA • KANAGAWA • AGE 26

YOSHIKO TAIRA • MIYAGI • AGE 19

MOTOKO • FUKUSHIMA • AGE 24

REIJI SAGAMI • SHIZUOKA • AGE 17

TAKU MISHIRO • TOKYO

P. PITOSHO • HIROSHIMA • AGE 17

F KYUU O • CHIBA

CHIYORI • TOKYO • AGE 19

KENTARO • TOKYO

SEIKO TSUTANO • OKAYAMA • AGE 25

MIKAGE • AKITA • AGE 19

SANDY • TAIWAN • AGE 21

SORAMARU • GUNMA

NANA BEATBALL • SAITAMA • AGE 14

SHOUKO • SAITAMA • AGE 15

SHOUKO • SAITAMA • AGE 15

TATSUYOSHI • EHIMA

SAGARA • KANAGAWA • AGE 20

ANN SAKURAGI • KAGOSHIMA • AGE 18

DAIDAI • KOCHI • AGE 22

HIRAHARA • MIYAZAKI • AGE 18

GEN • CHIBA • AGE 20

RYO HIZAKURA • AICHI

YASUHIRO AGETO • TOKYO • AGE 33

KAZUHA FUKAMI • TOKUSHIMA • AGE 21

KANDA • MIYAZAKI • AGE 30

MUTSUMI • IWATE

SUMITSUKI • CHIBA • AGE 16

YUMI SHIBATA • NAGANO • AGE 25

BASHI • MIYAGI

TAKAKO • SAITAMA • AGE 19

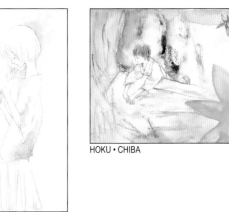

HOKU • CHIBA

KAITO KUROSAWA • MIE • AGE 20

SHINO • TOKYO • AGE 18

EISUKE • TOKYO

BUSHI DOU • NARA • AGE 20

NEKOASHI • OITA • AGE 15

ON TAKAHARA • TOCHIGI

KANOKO • NAGANO • AGE 19

KANA OHTSUKI • KYOTO • AGE 20

SHICHI • YAMAGUCHI • AGE 19

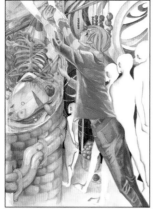

YAJU SHOUGETSU • KYOTO • AGE 16

NAOYA KUN • IBARAGI • AGE 20

MANANA HARUSAME • OSAKA • AGE 23

MITSUHA TOBIISHI • HOKKAIDO • AGE 20

KIRIYA MORI • KANAGAWA

HANATO • HYOGO • AGE 18

ERIZA KAMISHIRO • GUNMA • AGE 21

HIMATSUU • AICHI • AGE 20

KAZUYOSHI • NAGASAKI • AGE 23

JIUYEMOWU • TAIWAN • AGE 27

KEY • SAITAMA • AGE 46

KOSATO • TOKYO • AGE 21

KAZUYO YASUKAWA • TOYAMA

CHIZU • KYOTO

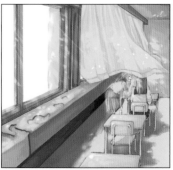

SHICHI • HOKKAIDO • AGE 16

YAMA NO AZA • OSAKA • AGE 17

SENRI JUUYA • TOKYO • AGE 19

NANATO • SAITAMA

AI • SHIGA • AGE 19

YOU • TOKYO • AGE 22

APRI • AGE 15

SPS • TAIWAN • AGE 22

WHEAT • HONG KONG • AGE 22

OUSHIN • SHIMANE • AGE 24

MIHIRO KOHARA • CHIBA • AGE 25

HAJIME MIZUKAZE • HYOGO • AGE 28

SOE • HIROSHIMA • AGE 23

YOTTSU • CHIBA • AGE 24

TAMARU NEKORI • TOKYO • AGE 20

MEIKUI • TAIWAN • AGE 13

MASAHIKO • OSAKA • AGE 22

HIROKAZU SASSA • TOKYO • AGE 21

KANITOU • TOKYO

337 • MALAYSIA • AGE 28

TSUO • TOKYO

YNORKA • TAIWAN • AGE 23

UCCA • MIE

NYAKI • EHIME • AGE 18

RINGO NAGANO • TOKYO

FUUKO TOMO • TOKYO • AGE 19

ITARU • SAGA

SAI • OSAKA • AGE 26

SPAWN MAX • TAIWAN • AGE 23

A-CHA • KYOTO • AGE 20

TONPUU NAKATA • OSAKA • AGE 16

YUMI KUSANO • TOKYO • AGE 19

XINCHEN • TAIWAN • AGE 19

KOMATSUBAME • KANAGAWA • AGE 16

MAKIHIKOU • HIROSHIMA • AGE 17

KATSUO • TOCHIGI

TAWAKO NIOKA • TOKYO

PAPARAYA • TAIWAN • AGE 22

POKO • FUKUOKA • AGE 17

ASUKA SUIRYUU • AICHI • AGE 20

MIRIN AMARUME • CHIBA • AGE 21

MATSUKERO • AOMORI • AGE 17

BENIKO • MIYAGI • AGE 20

MAI KIMURA • HOKKAIDO • AGE 19

YUMA GEKKA • AOMORI • AGE 17

SIR SHINO • MIE • AGE 16

AYA MASAKI • FUKUOKA

DODORUGEFU KAGUSHUUCHOU •
NAGANO • AGE 19

TSUKIKO TAKAMA • KANAGAWA

RIOKA • TOKYO • AGE 21

NOA • TOKYO

NEKOCHOU • TOYAMA • AGE 14

UENO • TOKYO • AGE 19

WAKABA • FUKUOKA • AGE 20

TOMO MUTSUKI • TOKYO

TESSEN • AOMORI • AGE 19

DOTAHACHI • CHIBA

KANRO • KANAGAWA • AGE 19

TOKIKAGE AKATSUKI • IWATE • AGE 17

HIMIKO ROSE • TOKYO

ABE SHIYOU • OITA • AGE 25

KIHARA • FUKUOKA • AGE 20

TSUBASA OKAJIMA • SAITAMA • AGE 23

JIN • TOYAMA

KOU • NAGANO • AGE 15

MUSHIMARU • MIYAGI • AGE 20

AI • YAMANASHI • AGE 17

MIKI • FUKUSHIMA

MASAKO • YAMAGUCHI • AGE 27

YANA • TOKYO

MASAYO OKADA • IBARAGI • AGE 30

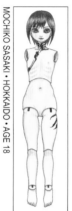
MOCHIKO SASAKI • HOKKAIDO • AGE 18

MA•JET • SAITAMA • AGE 21

KUUSAI HIRAI • HYOGO

HAIJI • MIYAGI

SAIMAKI • KANAGAWA • AGE 27

SAE YUUKI • FUKUOKA • AGE 20

RYOTA MATSUMOTO • TOKYO • AGE 20

SHINOBU • CHIBA • AGE 22

JOU GODOU • TOKYO • AGE 20

NOHOHO • TOKYO • AGE 20

SHIZUO GINIRO • AOMORI

KOUKO • YAMANASHI • AGE 17

KAHO SATOU • MIYAGI • AGE 17

AYA SATSUKI • HOKKAIDO • AGE 19

ITSUMI • TOKYO • AGE 17

HIBIKI SUIRA • OSAKA • AGE 19

AOI KITSUKI • KANAGAWA • AGE 25

MARIKO • YAMAGUCHI • AGE 15

MOEKO ODA • IWATE • AGE 16

NAGISAKO • SAITAMA • AGE 28

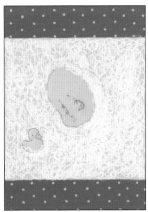

TSUGUMI KURO • TOCHIGI • AGE 21

MU • FUKUOKA • AGE 19

TAICHIRO • KYOTO • AGE 22

DOPPO • IWATE • AGE 17

KOTOMI SEO • MIYAGI • AGE 16

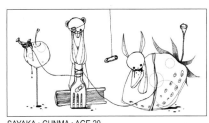

SAYAKA • GUNMA • AGE 20

MARIKO • YAMAGUCHI • AGE 15

AN • TOYAMA • AGE 18

KUZURE TORI • OSAKA • AGE 19

HIRONA TAKAHASHI • HOKKAIDO • AGE 17

SHICHIGEN • NAGASAKI

SAORI KUROSAKI • MIE • AGE 19

MARIO SUZUKI • SAITAMA • AGE 20

AQUA • TAIWAN • AGE 21

PING LAN HSIEH • TAIWAN • AGE 17

SATORU YASUI • TOKYO • AGE 27

KAYATORI -KAYA- • HIROSHIMA • AGE 17

AIZOME • FUKUSHIMA

SOUGETSU • IWATE • AGE 17

NANAFUSHI AKA KASAI KOUSUKE • AOMORI • AGE 19

SOUTA • NIIGATA • AGE 24

UKIMARU • AOMORI • AGE 17

JUNKO WATANABE • AICHI • AGE 22

KITSUNE SHIRATSUKI • NAGANO • AGE 19

SATOSHI ISANA • KYOTO

ELF • CANADA

HUIHUINIAN • TAIWAN • AGE 24

ANOU • FUKUOKA

JUUKU YOTSUGI • OSAKA • AGE 17

KUROTSUBAKI • HOKKAIDO

ERI KOGA • FUKUOKA • AGE 17

TANDAI • SHIGA • AGE 16

TOMO MUTSUKI • TOKYO

BANRI • CHIBA • AGE 16

RAKUTA • OSAKA • AGE 21

CHIHI • TOCHIGI • AGE 18

NORIKO ONCHI • OSAKA • AGE 26

YUU MAMEZAWA • CHIBA • AGE 19

KAYA • AICHI • AGE 19

AKI KANNO • YAMAGATA • AGE 22

KAZUKO TANIGUCHI • OKAYAMA • AGE 23

illustration by.wig 2004 un-stoic
KATSURA OF HARGON • KAGAWA • AGE 27

F.CP. • HONG KONG • AGE 23

F.CP. • HONG KONG • AGE 23

AKARI・AKITA

HOJOI • KYOTO • AGE 19

HIKOUKI • WAKAYAMA • AGE 22

YUKITO • HOKKAIDO

KOU KOTOBUKI • TOKYO

ITSUKI TATSUKIKAWA • OKINAWA • AGE 25

REN TIAN • TAIWAN • AGE 25

XI YI • TAIWAN • AGE 25

YOSHITSUGI • CHIBA

KOTO • KANAGAWA

ANOU • FUKUOKA

SATOKO SEGAWA • OSAKA

SHOJI YANAGI • SAITAMA

SUN HSIAO TIEN • TAIWAN • AGE 24

SETSU HAZUKI • HOKKAIDO • AGE 17

SUKEMARU ICHITA • TOKYO • AGE 20

TORIKO • OSAKA • AGE 29

EVAN • TAIWAN

SAZA • SAITAMA

MISATO • HOKKAIDO • AGE 18

YAMANEGURA • HYOGO • AGE 20

AOIN HATSU • TAIWAN • AGE 20

HOKU • CHIBA

CHINKO•SHONBORY • TOKYO • AGE 22

HSIANG KUO PING • TAIWAN

KASHIWAMO • TOKYO • AGE 18

NAKAMITSU • SHIGA

YUZUKI • TOKYO • AGE 20

KARASU • NAGANO

AKANE KAI • AICHI

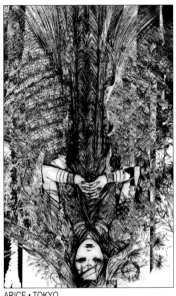

ARICE • TOKYO

MITSUKA CHIRU • KUMAMOTO

HIRAMARU • FUKUI • AGE 21

SHIRYUU NOZAKI • KANAGAWA • AGE 26

HARU KASUMI • TOKYO • AGE 27

HARUKO • CHIBA • AGE 16

KOKESHI • HYOGO • AGE 23

MACHI • SAITAMA • AGE 19

AONO • TOKYO • AGE 20

TAIKI • TOKYO • AGE 16

KEIICHI IBARAGI • EHIME • AGE 32

FUMINORI • KYOTO • AGE 17

NAO YAMAGATA • AOMORI • AGE 20

MATSUI • KOCHI

MOE TOWADA • NIIGATA • AGE 17

MAMI IRIYA • TOKYO • AGE 23

PENTA • SAITAMA • AGE 20

IKU • TOKYO • AGE 19

MARO • HOKKAIDO

MAKURA KABAA • HOKKAIDO • AGE 16

KENICHI • SAITAMA • AGE 17

HA-YASE • OSAKA • AGE 18

29 • TAIWAN • AGE 18

NAKI • KYOTO • AGE 22

SAKI • TOKYO • AGE 25

HITAKI • CHIBA

REIKAN SHOUNEN • OSAKA • AGE 17

CHIYA • NAGANO • AGE 17

CIELKANATA • OSAKA • AGE 21

AKIRA SHIJOU • TOKYO • AGE 20

KIWI • TAIWAN • AGE 23

USUKO • KUMAMOTO • AGE 15

MIAOYA • TOKYO • AGE 19

SORA HOZUMI • HYOGO • AGE 22

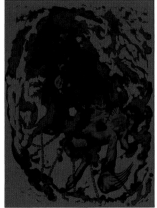

OKAKO • NARA • AGE 22

TAKAO RYOUTAROU • CHIBA • AGE 20

DOKU KINOKO • TOKYO • AGE 13

RANYA KUMAGAI • SAITAMA • AGE 27

YUUTA MIZUTANI • SHIZUOKA

YUTA CHIDORI • CHIBA

NATSUKI ASAKURA • KANAGAWA • AGE 21

ICHITA • OSAKA • AGE 20

TORI • HYOGO

LAN • TAIWAN • AGE 27

NAZUNA • AICHI

MANA • SAITAMA • AGE 17

KEIKO KURISU • FUKUOKA • AGE 31

FUUKO TOMO • TOKYO • AGE 19

NIKU • TOCHIGI • AGE 20

MUSHIMARU • MIYAGI • AGE 20

NANA MORITA • MIYAGI • AGE 22

YUMI INAZAKI • SAITAMA • AGE 17

KANKUROU JOUNOUCHI • HYOGO • AGE 22

ZENKEI • KUMAMOTO • AGE 21

KYOUKO MATSUMOTO • KANAGAWA • AGE 24

RYOU SAI • MIYAGI

KANGETSU KURONO • AKITA • AGE 15

KAGETSU • BEIJING • AGE 20

KOMATSUBAME • KANAGAWA • AGE 16

ODIE • TAIWAN • AGE 27

TOSHIBA • TAIWAN • AGE 23

TARUHO • MIYAGI

ERALIY • IBARAGI

KOINUMA • SAITAMA

CHIZU • KYOTO

YNORKA • TAIWAN • AGE 23

AKI KANNO • YAMAGATA

SHINIGAMI KUROU • CHIBA • AGE 17

RUI • SAITAMA • AGE 17

AYAKA TSUKUSHI • KYOTO • AGE 20

NOW TAKING SUBMISSIONS TO SS MAGAZINE!!

SS is looking for your art submissions. The materials you use and the motifs you choose are up to you. Don't hesitate to show the world as you wish to depict it. Character-based pieces, design-oriented works, mood pieces, or anything else are all fine. We welcome you experimenting and attempting new styles or trying out designs that are unusual for you. We'll ask the contributors of some of the very best pieces to create work for our opening pages and "Special Stage" sections, so please send in your stuff!

Also, if there were any artists you'd like to see a how-to on, just let us know!

FOR MORE DETAILS ON HOW TO SUBMIT, SEE THE BACK PAGE!

COLOR ILLUSTRATION SUBMISSIONS CORNER

Sky S

● Sky S takes color illustration submissions in 2 categories: "freestyle" illustrations, and "theme" illustrations.

1. In "Sky S Free" you can draw whatever you want.
2. "Sky S Theme" is themed. The theme for next issue will be "Girls of the World."

The size of your work can be anywhere from postcard to A4.

WE'LL BE WAITING!

BLACK & WHITE ILLUSTRATION SUBMISSIONS CORNER

Sea S

● We're taking illustrations, prose, and comics for our 8 sections of Sea S!

1. In "Sea S Sense" you draw whatever black & white illustration you want according to your own sensibility.
2. "Sea S Select" is a section where we select a different theme for each issue. Next issue's theme will be "Girls of the World."
3. In "S Stage" you draw any 1-page comic you wish. You can draw the 1-page comic on a single postcard.
4. "S Something" features 4-panel comics focusing on your present life or interests.
5. "S Story" features works that combine words and images. These are single pages which feature art as well as poetry, a monologue, or other lines.
6. "S Studio" features how to, materials, CG headaches, and questions.
7. "S Say" is a text section where you're free to talk about your recent events and interests.
8. "S Soul" features fan letters to SS contributors. As a present you will get an illustration in return!

The size of your work can be anywhere from postcard to A4.

● Where to send your art:
c/o "SS [your category]", Asukashin Corp., Kanda #3 Amerex Building, 3-10 Jimbocho, Kanda, Chiyoda-ku, Tokyo 101-0051

● You can send submissions for SpotS or GalleryS in SS's sister magazine Kikan <Quarterly> S in the same envelope. In those cases, please write "SS" on the back of all those pieces which are intended for SS.

● We also take electronic submissions:

● A picture resolution of 300dpi at actual size would be ideal. Any lower resolution might mean having to print at a smaller size in the magazine. Thank you for your understanding.

● When attaching the file to an e-mail, the data should be in compressed jpeg format no larger than 5MB. Any larger files should please be sent by a file storage website.

Special Stage

art · **SORAME**

art · MERINO WOOL

art · **KANNO AKI**

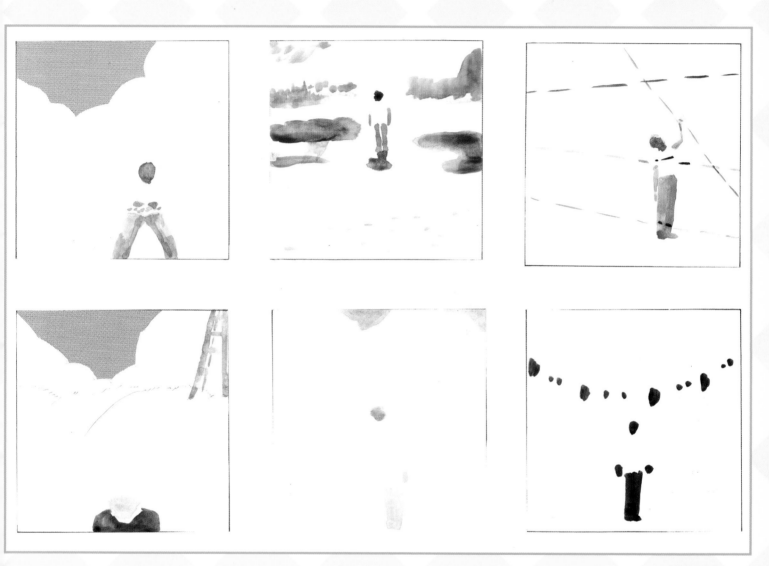

art · **MIHASHI**

art · **MARIMO**

病的 回路

MORBID CIRCUIT

カラス
KARASU

ノイズの音がうるさくてかなわない
THE NOISE IS SO LOUD I CAN'T STAND IT.

ヒトリアソビ

HANGING OUT BY MYSELF.

病的
（肉体や精神などが）
不健全で異常な様子.

MORBID:
{IN MIND AND BODY}
AN ABNORMAL STATE OF
UNWHOLESOMENESS.

回路
物質やエネルギーが
巡り回る道筋.

CIRCUIT:
A COURSE THROUGH WHICH
MATTER AND ENERGY CIRCULATE.

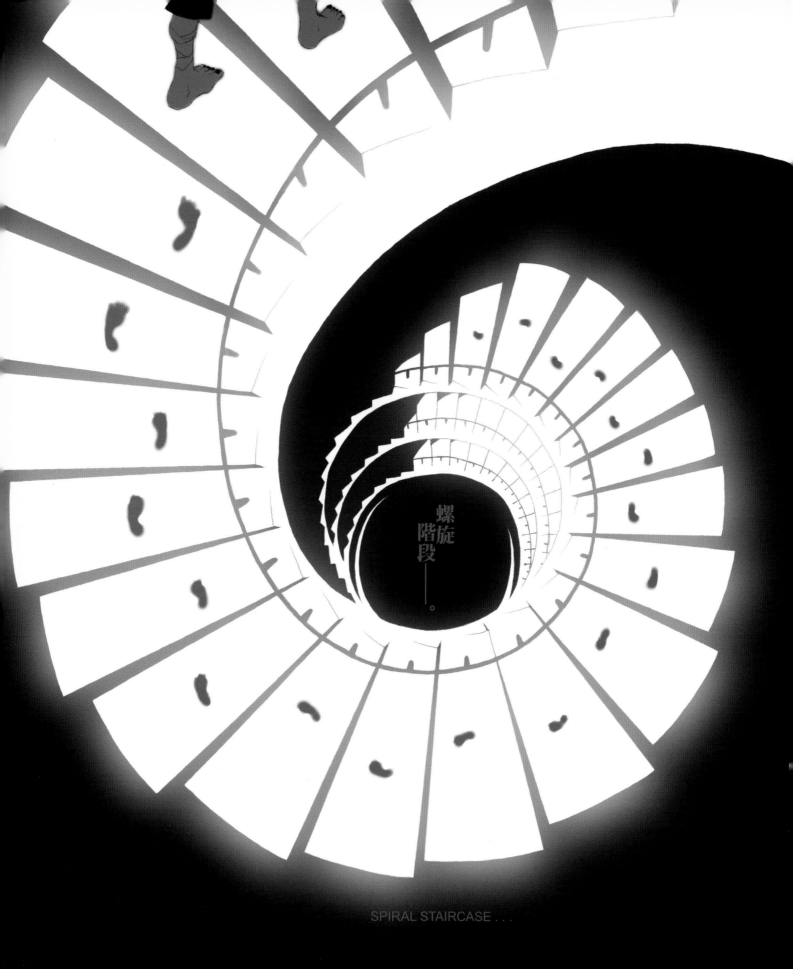

螺旋
階段
——
。

SPIRAL STAIRCASE . . .

懺悔は
13階より

REPENTANCE
FROM THE 13TH FLOOR

現実より逃避せよ

RETREAT
FROM REALITY

art · AOI

art · MINCHI

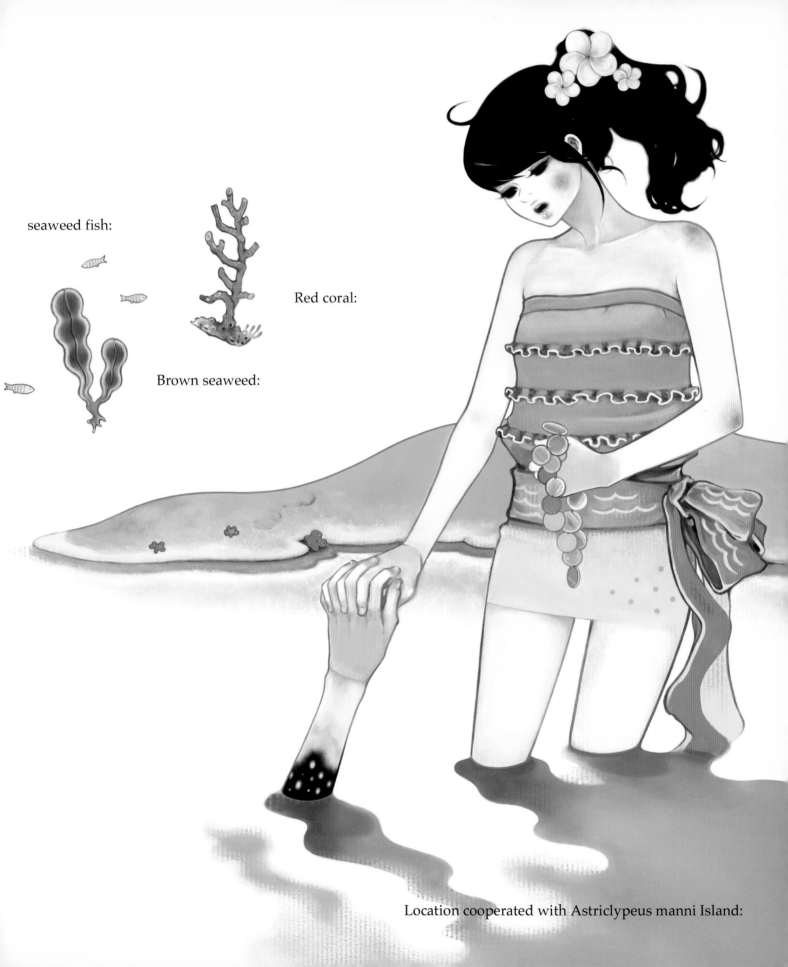

seaweed fish:

Red coral:

Brown seaweed:

Location cooperated with Astriclypeus manni Island:

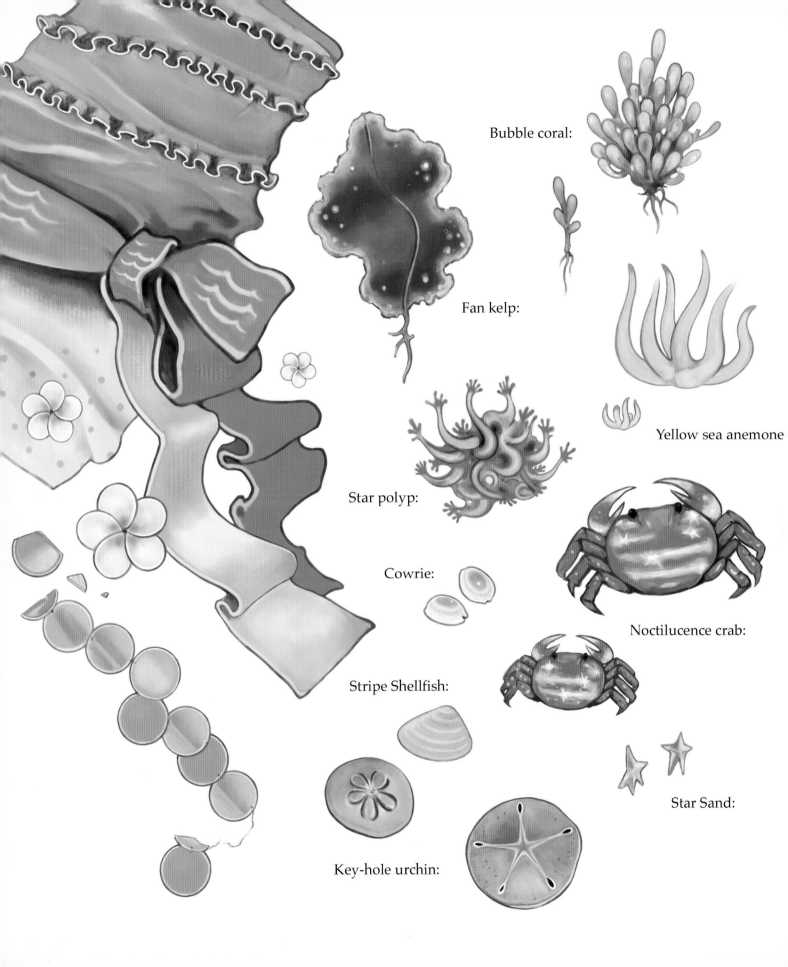

Bubble coral:

Fan kelp:

Yellow sea anemone

Star polyp:

Cowrie:

Noctilucence crab:

Stripe Shellfish:

Star Sand:

Key-hole urchin:

by Souichi

It was morning.

Outside the window

I saw myself in my youth.

He looked just like I remembered him,

And he looked at me reproachfully.

Almost as if he wanted to ask me

What I was doing in a place like this.

When I came to my senses

I saw my own tired face in the glass.

Is this a dream?

by Karintou

I saw the cracks in the world.

I saw souls destroyed.

I saw the first sun.

I saw the dying land.

I saw the scars of history.

I saw the white light of despair.

I saw the waving meridian.

I saw the horizon where the story ended.

I saw the instant when the roses withered and fell.

I saw the last moments of the empty stars.

I saw the atmosphere vanish.

I saw the finale of flames.

But whenever I look back, all I see is the color of the sky.

And that's the only thing.

by Ryuuya

The thing that closed that one box
Was a small child's white hand.
Did you forget?
Did you lose it?
Did you lose sight of it?

Can't you see it?
Holding onto brutally gentle memories
The box becomes a coffin
And the child's lost fragments are smothered in sleep.

by Yukito

I'm stopped on the way home.

The color of the sky cries out something

And soon the sun goes down in flames.

There's no end to running from the things that own us.

The heavy door is shut tight.

I fear the evening.

I fear the morning.

Sky burns.

Earth boils.

The men throw melancholy shadows on the way home.

A color you will never see again,

never remember again,

A red that sinks only in dreams.

by Sayaka Ouhito

When I was little,

I always used to go to a nearby abandoned

factory to play.

Things like broken pipes and mysterious junk

were very pretty, I thought as a kid.

And now that I'm older,

when difficult or sad times befall me,

I come back to this place.

It's remarkable how good it makes me feel.

Now I seem to remember, meeting some

special friend here

back when I was little.

No matter how hard I try, I can't remember

what kind of kid she was.

And when I sit down here,

I feel like maybe something's starting to come

back to me.

When was the last time I saw her?

NEED MORE INSPIRATION?

Check out these amazing books from Dark Horse!

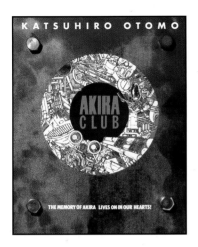

AKIRA CLUB
ISBN-10: 1-59307-741-6
ISBN-13: 978-1-59307-741-9
$29.95

COFFIN: THE ART OF VAMPIRE HUNTER D
ISBN-10: 1-59582-061-2
ISBN-13: 978-1-59585-061-7
$39.95

GUNGRAVE ARCHIVES
ISBN-10: 1-59307-522-7
ISBN-13: 978-1-59307-522-4
$19.95

INTRON DEPOT 1
ISBN-10: 1-56971-085-6
ISBN-13: 978-1-56971-085-2
$44.95

INTRON DEPOT 2: Blades
ISBN-10: 1-56971-382-0
ISBN-13: 978-1-56971-382-2
$44.95

INTRON DEPOT 3: Ballistics
ISBN-10: 1-59307-007-1
ISBN-13: 978-1-59307-007-6
$49.95

INTRON DEPOT 4: Bullets
ISBN-10: 1-59307-282-1
ISBN-13: 978-1-59307-282-7
$49.95

ROMAN ALBUM: Samurai Champloo
ISBN-10: 1-59307-642-8
ISBN-13: 978-1-59307-642-9
$17.95

WORLDS OF AMANO
ISBN-10: 1-59582-064-7
ISBN-13: 978-1-59582-064-8
$27.95

creating with technical pen
artist Karaya Mizore

Rotring is the name of a German art supply manufacturer, but it is used as a generic term for the technical pens that were used here. It's difficult to differentiate strong and weak lines with them, but they have an extra-fine, stable line quality that allows for uniformly fine lines and outstanding results. Technical pens are expensive, but you can easily draw extremely fine lines with them, and they are high-quality tools. In this article, we see how Kayara Mizore created this lovely and calm image using techical pens.

rough

First, we're going to trace this pencil rough over a lightbox. We just need a rough outline to start.

the boy's face

Mizore Karaya uses a lightbox to trace the rough drawing. However, lines which are simply traced from the rough seem dead and lack vitality, so you want to use the rough as no more than a reference or "target," working almost as if you're drawing the picture for the first time. The reason for tracing is that because the pen lines are so thin, if you tried to erase pencil lines underneath them, you could take out the pen lines, too. So instead we draw over the rough directly in pen. As you can see from the pictures, keep turning the page around to angles that are easy to draw in.

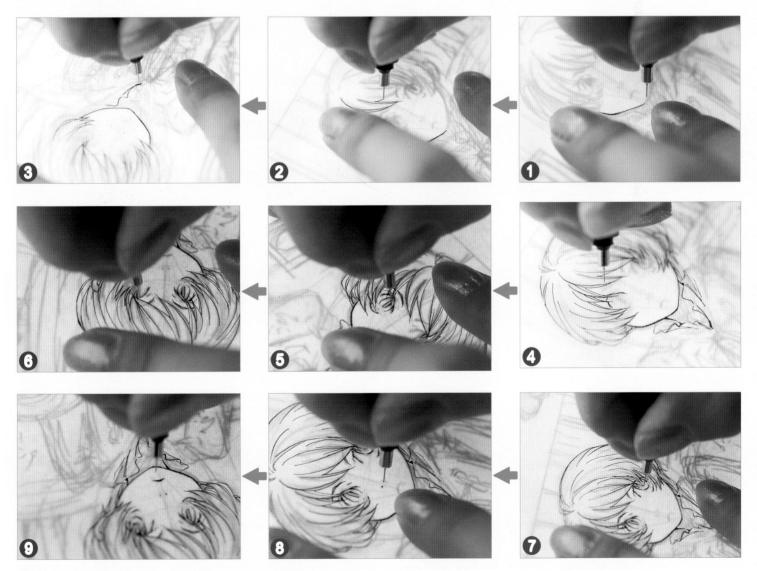

the boy's vest

There are some laces tied together on the boy's vest. First, using the rough as a reference, put in marks as guides for holes where the laces would come out. Next, to create the laces, draw the ribbon and draw lines to each side leading to the holes where the laces come out. After drawing the hooks that the laces are pulled through, draw the patterns on the fringe lace beside them. As you can see from the pictures, the tips of tech pens are as thin as needles. As a result they can be used to draw things like laces and other finely detailed adornments with even line weights.

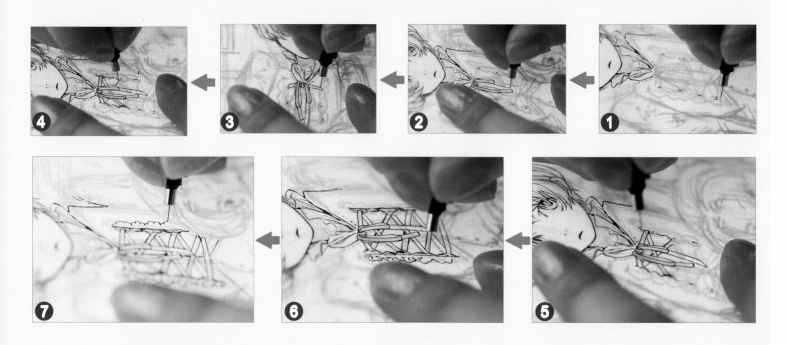

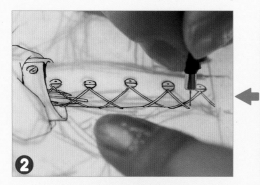

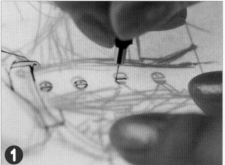

the boy's boots

The boots also have laces. As above, first put in guiding marks for where the laces will come out. Then draw laces leading from them, but much thinner this time. The good thing about tech pens is that you can draw lines this close without them running into each other. Even places where laces cross the ones below them can be depicted to accurately look that way. Finally, to give the boots that sense of volume unique to leather, add slanted lines to create solidity.

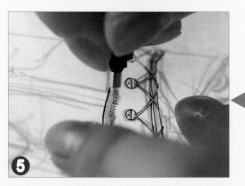

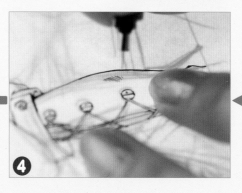

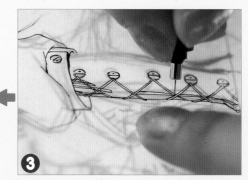

the stuffed toy

The stuffed toy has patches of fluffy hair. If you draw in the lines too clearly, you won't get the sense of that fluff. In these areas, don't connect lines to create an outline, but just put in fine lines like individual points. Thanks to the light box you can see the guiding lines underneath, so use the pen to follow the curves of the stuffed toy and draw in point-like fluff. The seams and tears and twisted, dangling string can also be expressed in detail here.

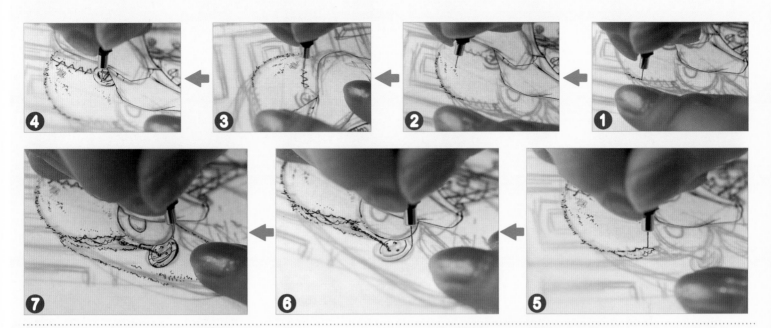

the completed picture

Looking at the finished image, we can see how the fabric of the clothes, the stuffed toy, the chair, and the cabinet at the back have all been given different textures just by the lines used. The fine points were all drawn by hand to suitably express their delicacy and give the image depth. These might not be the best tools for vigorous action scenes, but we recommend that those who like to work slowly towards carefully constructed pieces try technical pens at least once.

crosshatching the chair

To make the chair appear dark, we use crosshatching. Karaya Mizore did the entire picture only with line work and without screentone, so even shadowed areas are just lines bunched together to make the area darker. To give this rough area some nuance, lines are piled on top of each other to avoid homogenous single lines. The crosshatched lines are not uniformly straight either. They have a little shakiness to them. The point is to draw every line and not use screentone. Gradually increase it in the same way to make the crosshatched area larger. Even a picture that's composed only of black and white lines can be given texture and depth if you put care into the fine details.

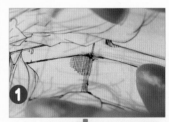

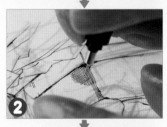

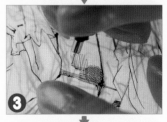

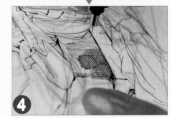

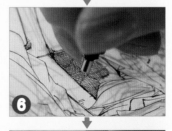

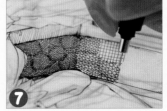

creating with screentone
artist Touya Senri

Touya Senri uses crow quills and G-Pens to create her line drawings and then lays down solid areas of screentone. There are many varieties of screentone available these days, but Senri uses IC brand tone. In this article she uses orthodox screentone, which can be scraped away and produces a wide range of effects.

Ink the hair in the same way with a crow quill. Rotate the page into positions in which lines are easier to draw out.

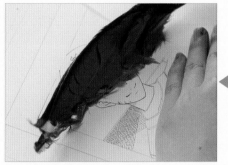

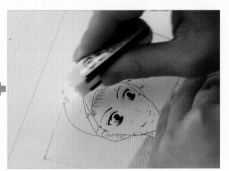

Once you're done inking, erase the pencil, then brush away the shavings.

the fence

Use a crow quill for the fence in the background, and use a ruler to guide your lines. First draw all the slanting lines in one direction, and be sure they don't end up intersecting by keeping an even space between them. Now do the crossing wires the same way by following along the ruler with strong and weak areas, and you'll end up with the nuance of overlapping wires in the fence.

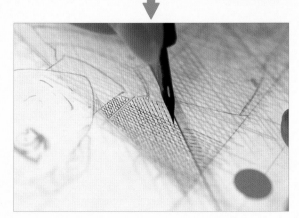

inking

We're going to start by inking over the pencil line drawing. Go over the lines with a crow quill to create eyelashes, and to create the effects of light in the irises, draw in gradations with slanted lines. Build up these lines at the bottom, which will be darker—the top will be lighter. Fill in the pupil with a brush pen. The X mark you see in the photo is a mark used in comics to indicate areas that need to be completely filled in with black.

①

②

③

④

⑤

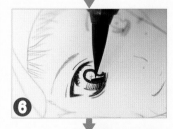
⑥

⑦

filling in the hair

The hair is filled in solidly with a brush pen. First put in a thick line at the edge of the hat, then work down from it to the tips of the hair. Do the thinnest bits last with a millipen. This one's a High-tec.

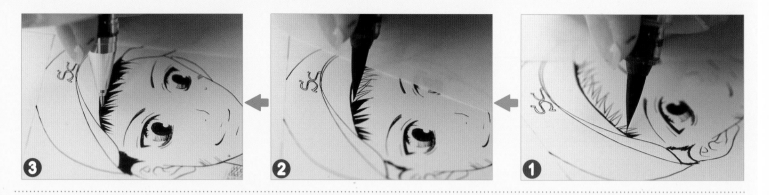

crosshatching the arm

Fill in the solid blacks again, and in the parts left white we'll add crosshatching. First, draw out uniform slanted lines, then shift the angle a bit and add more slanted lines the same way. Add another layer for dark areas, creating smooth gradations of shadow.

screentoning the clouds

Use a cutter to shave out "enclosures." The middle of these enclosures will also be left intact. These will be the color of the sky. The edge of the cutter in the photo is flat. By creating randomly strong and weak areas, a shading effect is produced.

Use a pencil to draw in a general guideline of what you'd like to cut out. The screentone inside this area will be left as is.

We're going to create the gradation of the clouds with screentone. As you can see above, we're using a dark grade. Lay down a solid layer to start.

Again, shave with the tip of the blade. Thanks to the layering of screentone, the indistinct gradation of the clouds will become smoother. Because we've layered two levels of screentone—one dark and one light—after shaving you will find places with very little mesh, other places where you've cut diagonal lines with the blade tip, etc. and this complicated mix of effects all create the delicate tones of the sky.

After you're done cutting, paste on another layer of screentone. This one will be a light grade. Be careful not to sandwich in any shavings from the last job.

Shave with the tip of the blade. The blade should cut very sharply. Cutting fine, diagonal lines in this manner is an effective technique.

screentoning the boy's face

4 Use the tip of the blade to peel off the unneeded parts. In the case of very complex shapes, you need to be careful that the needed areas don't get caught and torn away too.

3 To get rid of any unnecessary parts, cut into them with a utility blade. You should have a general idea of which parts these will be from the line drawing itself.

2 This is what it looks like pasted on. The possibility exists that some air or wrinkles have gotten in, so it's necessary to check it thoroughly.

1 First, put screentone over only the area you need. Put down the edge of one side first, and use a cutter or something to help paste it down without letting any wrinkles form.

7 First, paste the needed volume onto the page. When layering screentone, you can sometimes end up with a moiré effect (a strange optical effect caused by the layering of lines or dots), so you need to be careful that the line screen is the same and that they are set at the same angles.

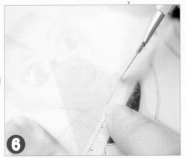

6 Before adding the next layer, you need to see how much of the next screentone you will need. Put the tone against the picture, and mark it for the size.

5 After you've pulled off the unnecessary sections, go over the remaining areas again to make sure they're pasted down firmly.

9 Now that the needed parts are holes in the sheet, lift off the tone you pasted down again and the unnecessary sections will come off. Now it's complete.

8 To again remove any unnecessary pieces, we put "gaps" in it. The nose, the mouth, and the depression under the mouth are the toned parts this time. It's normal to use layering like this to create detailed tones.

---

the completed picture

Students on the baseball team are just finishing up as evening settles in. There's the sense that they're washed in backlighting, thanks to the characters being entirely shadowed with screentone. The clouds were also created by shaving away screentone, a technique that gives them the effect of unevenness in their formation. Screentone can be used for many purposes as well as creating different textures and lighting. See what kinds of effects you can get out of them.

One Point!
how to hold the cutter when shaving

Shave with the edge of the cutter flat. This edge isn't sharp, so it's more like you're scraping away with it. If you put power into the edge, you can create rough scrapings.

When using the tip of the blade, don't hold it too close to the tip, and just hold the handle. This way you won't put too much strength in it, and there's no worry of ripping the paper. This way you can cut smooth, crisp lines.

There are many different types of pens available for doing black & white illustration. They each have their own feel, and they produce an infinite variety of results. It would be great if we all had the time to try them all out for ourselves to see which was the best fit for us. To that end, Fumika and Sukemaru Ichita have tried out a bunch of pens for us. In some cases it was their first time to use them, and some others were new discoveries entirely. If one sounds just right for you, be sure to try it out!

Copic Multiliner

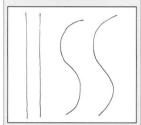

Regular millipens and felt-tip pens blend or bleed if you write over them with marker, but the Copic Multiliner is a remarkable millipen that doesn't bleed if drawn over with other Copic. Several manga artists use them as their primary tool for illustration. When dry they become waterproof and alcohol resistant. Their tips don't get clogged up like ballpoints, and they're stable to work with. In this issue's how-to with Babiry, this was her primary tool.

Fumika: "The markers felt extra-fine, so of course they had to be Copics. They're geared to creating clear lines with just a touch. For those who like clean lines, these allow that unique Copic texture. I feel like the color came out comparatively lighter."

Rotring

When it comes to accurate, extra-fine pens, the German company Rotring is unparalleled with their drafting tools. Their original concept was to create a fountain pen that didn't leak, and their endurance is outstanding. The pen's tip is needle-like and so fine it would be easy to prick your finger with it. The price is vastly different than for millipens, but to draw the finest lines, there is no other choice. The sizes go up bit by bit from 0.1 to 0.13 to 0.18 to 0.2, so you can count on the pen for any level of detailing. In the manga world, Maki Kusumoto uses them, and they are a very cool tool.

Fumika: "Fine and lovely. They're similar to Copic's Multiliner, but the pen tip is harder and easy to work with. It's so thin, in fact, that you can write tiny letters with it. It made me want to buy one. I wonder how long the ink and tip will last . . . "

Pigma

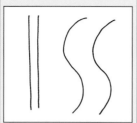

This is a felt-tip pen manufactured by Sakura. The 0.05 mm to 0.3 mm range are their millipen line. However, since they're felt tip, a 0.05 won't actually come out that thin on paper. They come out in thick, even colors, and the uniform feel is attractive. They are water soluble, but once they dry they're waterproof. Taiyo Matsumoto used to finish his artwork with Pigma, and they are quite popular in the comics industry. Hiroaki Samura does most of his inking with Pigma.

Fumika: "The lines came out thicker than I expected given the tip thinness, but if you work softly you can get thinner lines. I like that they didn't get scratchy even if I worked quickly. They're kind of like markers."

HI-TEC-C

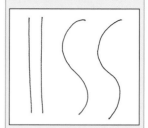

This is a ball-point pen made by Pilot which many people use to write text, but a lot of other people also use for illustration. The 0.3 millimeter is useful and can be bought anywhere, but recently they've released a nanotech level 0.25 mm ball—the world's smallest. It's remarkable they've managed to make pens this thin while maintaining the low price. The only problem with such fine pens is they tend to get clogged up easily. In those cases there's nothing you can but buy a new one. The ink isn't dissolved by markers and vice versa, which also makes them popular.

Ichita: "I've been using these pens since I was in junior high school. They were great for taking notes. I use the 0.25 mm now, and the tips of mine don't stop up very much, so they're quite handy. Before I buy them, I always test them out first. The ones that seem to test out okay and look good usually don't get clogged, and I use them till they run out."

mechanical pencil

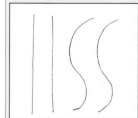

Everyone has used a mechanical pencil to draw with at least once, meaning that they're the tool everyone's probably most used to. They come out very light if you print them, so most people don't use them to create final art. The comic Manmaru created for this issue was done with pencil, and there are a lot of artists who like pencil drawings. Hiroaki Samura has said that, as you'd expect, pencils are one of the only tools he uses. You can use them for actual gentle gray gradations, so super-detailed artists like Tatsuyuki Tanaka and Ryuichiro Kutsuzawa almost always work through stages of mechanical pencil.

Fumika: "I used to use 0.5 leads, but when I switched to 0.3 I found it much more useful. I use a B lead because you don't need to put as much power into it to work with as an HB. And if you do put strength into it, it comes out really thick, so you can widen lines or black out entire areas easily."

writing brush	brush pen	crow quill	G-Pen	New Nib School-G
		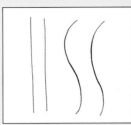	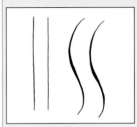	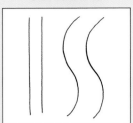

	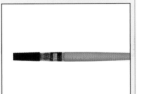			

writing brush

Also used with color, the writing brush is a basic art tool. Many people use it for black & white work. It produces a somehow austere image—the sense of pop design is not strong here—but it's actually extremely functional. The great Taiwanese master Chen Uen, respected by Pin Fan and Chen Shu-Fen, said: "A single brush can paint the very thinnest lines and the very thickest." Well, the very thinnest lines certainly come from the writing brush. Of course, it takes a great level of expertise to actually produce them . . . It's hard to create a stable line, but the ways you hold the brush and the ways you move it produce entirely different effects. Light and dark can be modulated. And if you go to the extreme, you can create a truly deep vision of the world.

Fumika: "I got the impression this brush was easier to work with than the brush pen. If I'd had a brush of higher quality, it might have turned out even better. I did this picture with a cheap 367 yen brush. It's good I was able to do the solids and toning all with one brush."

brush pen

A text brush that is used in every Japanese household for writing New Year's cards. Because it's so handy, it's an easy choice whenever you want a brush effect. The ink keeps flowing out of it, so it's easy to have a constantly thick stroke, but then the opposite is also true that you can't use it for light painting. Also the tip gets bad relatively quickly. However, it's unlike a normal brush, which has a soft tip that is difficult to work with, but it has the touch of a brush and that sustained relaxed feel. Akihiro Yamada often uses a brush pen.

Ichita: "I was stunned when I saw Ringo Yamada create a picture of flowing lines with a brush pen—it was a crash course. It's easy to create strong or weak lines with, and I was fascinated at its range of solid fills to fine lines. The brush pen I use has waterproof pigment inks, so even if you paint over previous coats they don't melt, so it can be put to many uses."

crow quill

These were originally used to draw contour lines on maps, so as you'd expect, they produce thin lines. As with the G-Pen, it has become an almost generic term for pens that are used to draw manga with. They're often used for their fine line quality and detailing, especially of backgrounds. And, of course, the line can be made stronger or weaker depending on the amount of pressure exerted. The delicate lines of manga artists like Yuuichi Kumakura and Kaoru Fujiwara are all done with crow quill.

Fumika: "After working with it for a little bit, the nib split. The imperfections added a certain flavor to the work, like my own vague lines. I felt like you could draw softer with it than a G-Pen."

G-Pen

This pen was originally intended for writing text but has become popular in Japan as a manga pen. The nib is soft, so lines tend to come out thick. For this reason it's used mainly for characters and other objects that need to appear prominent. When used well, the G-Pen can produce a pronounced range of strong to weak lines. That said, you couldn't say, for example, that all of Kosuke Fujishima's fine lines could be entirely done with a G-Pen. Because it's so soft, as long as the paper is smooth and soft enough, it will easily execute elegant curves.

Ichita: "The nib was soft, so I could draw strong and weak lines and they were always different, which was interesting. Since it's a dip pen, it's a tool you could also use with colored inks to create color illustrations."

New Nib School-G

Made by Tachikawa, this nib is frequently used in manga, but it's not the type that needs to be constantly dipped in ink—it's a cartridge. So, amazingly, you can keep working without stopping for ink. The feel of the line is somewhere between the School Pen and G-Pen. It uses manga pigment inks. It generally produces lines of strong or weak thickness between 0.2 and 0.5 mm. Tachikawa also has a product called "New Nib School," but this one is considerably thinner.

Ichita: "I don't use dip pens to draw with so I used this with a bit of trepidation. You can use it as soon as you take off the cap, so it was much easier to use than an actual dip pen. The ink is waterproof so you could use it for color illustration as well."

sea SCHOOL

monochrome illustration collection

Everyone got to draw whatever they wanted for our first issue. Starting next issue, this section will be split up into categories, so keep sending in your work!

YUIBI • CHIBA • AGE 21

AKANE KAI • AICHI

PARU • TOKYO • AGE 18

DOPPO • IWATE • AGE 18

FUMIKA • TOKYO

MAIKO • KANAGAWA

RISA YOSHIARA • HOKKAIDO • AGE 18

RIKO • KAGAWA • AGE 21

MAREO TAROU • KOCHI • AGE 23

NITORO KUSANO • TOKYO • AGE 18

CHISAN • OSAKA • AGE 16

TESSEN • AOMORI • AGE 19

KOUKO • YAMANASHI • AGE 17

JIIKU • KANAGAWA • AGE 26

SOURAKU • KANAGAWA • AGE 20

MATSUKERO • AOMORI • AGE 17

SHUICHI GENOUKOKU • HOKKAIDO • AGE 17

TSUBASA OKAJIMA • SAITAMA • AGE 23

SORA HOZUMI • HYOGO • AGE 22

KANOKO • NAGANO • AGE 19

MR. MEGANE • TOKYO • AGE 19

JUUKU YOTSUGI • OSAKA • AGE 17

JIKIDARIA • OKINAWA • AGE 14

SHIGETATSU • TOKYO • AGE 26

MIYAKO • CHIBA

AYA MASAKI • FUKUOKA

MARIKO • YAMAGUCHI • AGE 15

FUYU MITSU • AOMORI • AGE 18

KIHARA • IWATE • AGE 17

DODORUGEFU KAGUSHUUCHOU • NAGANO • AGE 19

KOU • NAGANO • AGE 15

YOUBANA MIZUYA • AOMORI • AGE 19

KOUKO • YAMANASHI • AGE 17

HIRUMA KOZUE • TOKYO • AGE 22

TRASH • CHIBA • AGE 22

AKIRA SHIJO • TOKYO • AGE 20

YUKOU HAEMOTO • YAMAGUCHI

JOU GOMAMOTO • FUKUI

NEKOCHOU • TOYAMA • AGE 14

KIHARA • IWATE • AGE 17

MATSUI • KOCHI

YUIBI • CHIBA • AGE 21

PARU • TOKYO • AGE 18

KAZUKO TAKEDA • CHIBA • AGE 53

MIZUTAKI • MIYAGI • AGE 16

TOMO MUTSUKI • TOKYO

MAGNITUDE 6.6 • AICHI • AGE 19

MITSURU • SHIGA

JUUYA SENRI • TOKYO • AGE 19

YAOTO • SHIZUOKA • AGE 18

SHIYA • NAGANO • AGE 17

ASUKA SUZUKI • HOKKAIDO • AGE 22

HIROKAZU UEMATSU • SHIZUOKA • AGE 24

YUKI SAKAMOTO • CHIBA • AGE 16

SAKI • TOKYO • AGE 18

RAKURAKU KUSA • SAGA • AGE 18

MATSUI • KOCHI

HARUKA KATASE • KANAGAWA • AGE 22

MJS • NAGANO

SHIZUO GINIRO • AOMORI

SHIZUO GINIRO • AOMORI

SUKEMATSU INASAKI • SATAMA • AGE 17

SHUN • KOCHI • AGE 15

BOM • SAITAMA • AGE 27

ASANA SAKIOKA • YAMANASHI • AGE 20

MUSHIMARU • MIYAGI • AGE 20

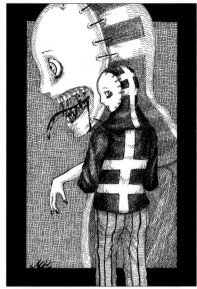

MAI KIMURA • HOKKAIDO • AGE 19

TOHO ONDA • SAITAMA • AGE 17

AKIKA • TOKYO • AGE 15

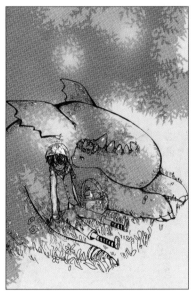

MARIO SUZUKI • SAITAMA • AGE 20

YASUKI • KOCHI • AGE 15

KAZEYUKI KIRANO • NAGASAKI • AGE 16

KAZUNE HIBIKINO • OSAKA

SAYAKA IKEDA • TOKYO • AGE 25

ZARAME • NARA • AGE 23

ITSUMI • TOKYO • AGE 17

NORUKA SORUKA • AICHI • AGE 15

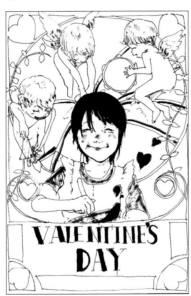

MAARU • AICHI

NAOYA SHINOSAKI • OSAKA • AGE 16

HA-YASE • OSAKA • AGE 18

AOI SAME • IBARAGI • AGE 24

AQUARIUM • NAGASAKI • AGE 17

Special Stage

art · **KAGEKYU**

art · **MERUMERU**

art · **AYAME**

art · **TAGA**

art · **DOKUHO**

art · **SEIKA HISUI**

(Love Fortune)   (Capsule toy backgammon)
(Series)
(What will you get?)

CAPSULE TOY BACKGAMMON
by MANMARU

(You have begun your relationship and are on the second square.
To move ahead, roll the dice and proceed according to the number.)

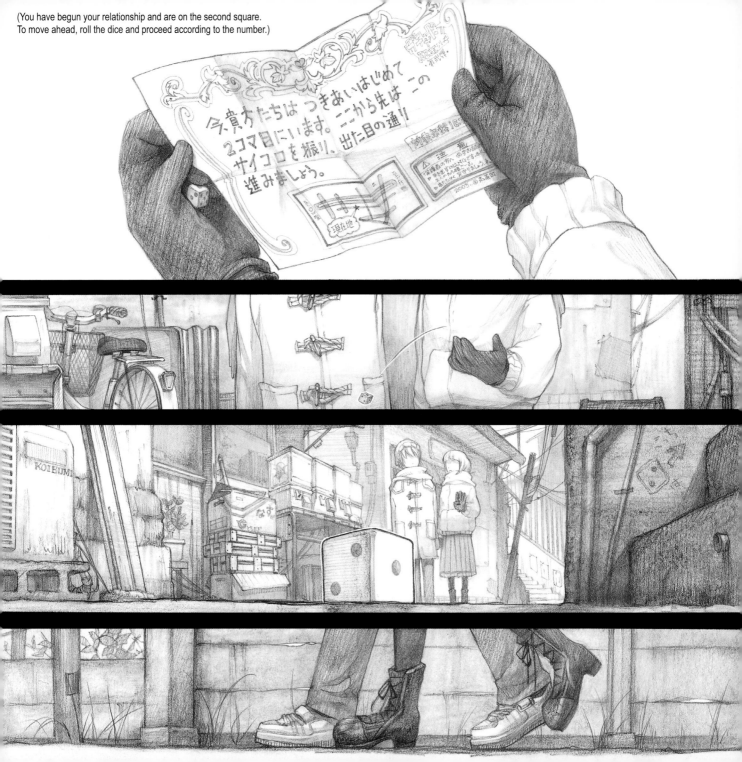

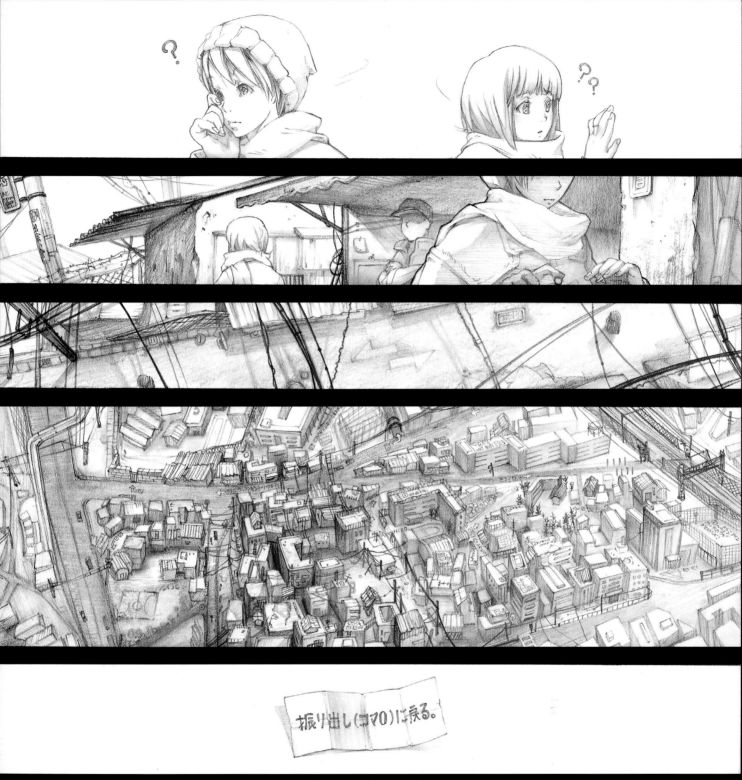

Return to start (square zero).

終

STYLE SCHOOL — THE ARTIST'S HEART

In this section S-0 answers questions that S-chan is worried about. S-chan has just started drawing pictures, so there's a lot of stuff she doesn't understand.

 Hey, S-0! I want to draw a sailor uniform . . . Do you have any good photo references?

 Are you drawing a student?

 Yeah. I've got this image of a girl in a sailor suit hanging around in a tunnel. I thought I'd like to draw a picture of it.

 Aha . . . I see. Anything else?

 When I think about it more, I'm not sure how the ribbon would be knotted on a sailor uniform and whether the hem of the top would be scrunched or straight. So I thought I'd ask you for a photo reference.

 S-chan, it's too soon to go looking for a photo.

 Yeah, but I want to draw it now! You've got things I can use to make models with and things to make costumes . . . They come right out of your chest, right?

 S-chan, aren't you mistaking me for a different robot . . .? First of all, if you wanted to ask for useful tools from the future, wouldn't you just ask for a pen that makes you draw well and be done with it?

 No! I want to draw with my own skill!

 So which is it?! If you want to draw it yourself, then don't ask me for references! I meant to tell you this before. Any time you're just walking around you should take a good look at anything you're worried about drawing. For example, if you're thinking about sailor uniforms, you can see them all over the place, right?

 Well, that's true, but when I'm actually drawing, it's more effective to actually have pictures with me to look at.

 But photos have their weak points. A photo is taken under certain conditions, so if it's outdoors, then the strength of the lighting depends on where the sun is. And if it's indoors, the lighting will determine the direction of the shadows and their strength. As long as someone took the photo, then it's a "work," a deliberately controlled image. That photographer specifically wanted to create that image under those conditions.

 I know that, but . . .

 So a photo that captures that one unique moment will have very few circumstances in common with the image you want to draw. If you ignore that and still use it as a reference, there will be flaws in the position of the light and solidity, and your drawing may come out very flat, a superficial copy.

These are pictures of "Gunkanjima" in Nagasaki, taken some time back by *Style School*'s editorial department. The island is entirely an abandoned ruin, a ghost town, and is very difficult to land on these days. Such a scene can be seen only in photographs, but predictably these photos do nothing to capture the sheer awe of the place. The *SS* staff members who actually went there said the power of the place was so overwhelming it made them shiver, something you could only experience at the actual site. It's that rush that will really put magical energy into a picture when it's being made. So even when using these as reference, you can put your imagination to work more than usual, but if you haven't experienced it for yourself, the picture will probably come out less inspiring than the reality.

 Argh! S-0, you don't mince words, do you? I'm just a beginner, so can't I use photo references for study?

 So, if you get a picture of a tunnel but there's no person inside it, then what? And even if there is a person, it won't be right for you unless the person's the right size.

 I guess you're right, but . . . I don't understand perspective, so if I try to put a person in there, I won't know which size is correct.

 No matter the size of the tunnel, even if you understand the measurements, that won't capture the size, will it?

 I see. So even if it was a twenty-meter tunnel, how can I convey that length? I've only been through a tunnel in a car, and it only takes a second.

 And if you try to capture it in a photo, you'll only catch 0.008 seconds of it. 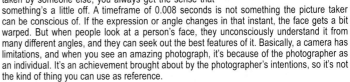 If you ever look at a photo of you taken by someone else, you always get the sense that something's a little off. A timeframe of 0.008 seconds is not something the picture taker can be conscious of. If the expression or angle changes in that instant, the face gets a bit warped. But when people look at a person's face, they unconsciously understand it from many different angles, and they can seek out the best features of it. Basically, a camera has limitations, and when you see an amazing photograph, it's because of the photographer as an individual. It's an achievement brought about by the photographer's intentions, so it's not the kind of thing you can use as reference.

 Awww . . . you're sooo strict! So what do I do?!

 In my opinion, you need to see things with your own eyes and write down notes and sketches of the things that strike you. You may not be aware of it yourself, but in the moment you witness something, you will be affected by things like your feel of the season, the temperature, the atmosphere of the place, smells, and clothes. The main thing is that whatever "thoughts" you get from to draw a picture with are not all of which the picture is composed. A lot of pros who draw nice pictures sketch people. This means drawing a lot, which is important, but also drawing to remember the sensations at that particular moment. While something is moving you so deeply, you draw it and commit it to memory. S-chan, you've got the free time, so if you want to draw a girl in a sailor suit hanging around a tunnel, I think the best thing to do is go to a tunnel and physically sense the darkness, the dampness, the lonely atmosphere. Try to imagine a girl in a sailor suit standing there, and have fun with it.

 It's seems like work but sounds fun, too.

 Either way, it's not a picture you can draw quickly, so it's best not to be in a rush and go straight to photo references hoping they'll make you a better artist.

 You could have put it nicer, but I see the main point is the attitude.

 Your feeling is what's important. Even if your technique is not realistic, the picture can communicate your message. The father of illustration, the American Howard Pyle, said something like, "If you're going to draw people digging a hole, first you need to dig one yourself. Once you've experienced it, you'll know what it feel like to do it and you have to put that emotion into the picture." Of course, personally experiencing it is not that important, but the level of feeling is. What you can't experience for yourself you can imagine, so in a sense if you're looking for reference, movies might be better than still photos. Some artists will watch a movie several times over and then recall it from memory as they're working. The act of remembering resembles the act of imagining, I guess. Also, it might be okay to go to a location, get a sense of it, and photograph it yourself. This isn't a technical reference, but just a "clue" to help you remember things, like, "Ah! This part was cool!"

 Okay! I get it! I need to go see a tunnel! S-0, do you have a magic door that can teleport me anywhere?

That's . . . that other robot again . . .

after SCHOOL

Next month (as I write this), May 2007, will be the nineteenth anniversary of the first manga Dark Horse published in English—Kazuhisa Iwata's *Godzilla*, his graphic novel of the Japanese monster film originally titled *Gojira 1984*. Thanks to many years of effort by our editors and adaptation staff, and most especially because of the longtime commitment to this field by our past associate Studio Proteus, Dark Horse today is the second oldest publisher of manga in the United States, and it wasn't for lack of desire that we aren't the first—we tried to get the rights to *Lone Wolf and Cub* back in 1987. That story, too, had a happy ending, as years later, we *did* get it, completing the never-finished English version of the series and seeing it become a best-seller with almost a million copies out there. It was a deserving, but all the more remarkable achievement for a thirty-year-old manga drawn for an adult readership, full of crusty old samurai and with no anime or videogame tie-ins, and even *flopped*—why, it seems to break all the rules.

There's an explanation, and it's fairly simple. *Lone Wolf and Cub* is enormously successful not because it's an example of (local TV news voice) *that hot new format known as "main-gah,"* not because it's in a surefire genre (there are other, quite deserving samurai manga which haven't succeeded in the U.S. market), and certainly not because it was promoted through a professional ad agency sniffing after the next big thing (forget "main-gah;" I once sat through a speech by a publicity firm whose rep confidently spoke—again and again—of what they could do to boost the sales of "magna"), but because it's a powerfully considered and created vision from two individual Japanese artists—writer Kazuo Koike and the late artist Goseki Kojima. Oh, yeah, and have you noticed something else? *Lone Wolf and Cub*, one of the bestselling manga ever in the English-language market, isn't really drawn in "the manga style."

You and I know what people mean when they talk about "the manga style." And the same concept sometimes gets bandied about in Japan, too; after all, many of the "how to draw manga" books currently out there are direct translations of Japanese editions. This magazine, *Style School*, is coming from the same locale, but a very different place. Like Kazuo Koike's own famous instruction school

for creators—whose most famous graduate, Rumiko Takahashi, revolutionized *shonen* (boys') manga by bringing a feminine wit to it—*Style School* isn't telling you to pattern yourself only on what was done before, but to become an artist of possibilities, rather than merely models. There's a reason why people who are thought of as drawing in the "manga style," such as Katsuhiro Otomo, Moyoco Anno, and Yasuhiro Nightow (themselves very different in style!), all admire Katsuya Terada—whose *Monkey King* adaptation is published through Dark Horse—another manga artist who usually isn't thought of as "manga style." It's again because, like *Style School*, Terada is after the larger possibilities of illustration and painting, not because he's snooty or academic, but so that he can bring it back home to the manga world and inject it with new charisma and panache.

It's been said that every aspiring artist has a thousand bad drawings or paintings within them, and the sooner you get them done and out of your way, the better. The articles in *Style School* will, I believe, give you the right kind of perspective, values, and encouragement. You may, as many fans of Japanese illustration do, also want to lay hands on and use the same brand tools that the Japanese artists do—there's a certain energy just in that, like having a sacred sword in your grip. But you're going to have to go ahead, to use this magazine and use whatever tools, and then *work hard at it for years*. And here's the point: to the artist, this is a kind of work which has a purpose and is meaningful to you—the kind of work that is worth doing.

You should do it, so get to work. Work hard to develop a style; try to *be* stylish (like CLAMP or Paul Pope), but don't let anyone ever tell you what a "manga style" looks like—*Style School* certainly won't. Give the world your answer through your work: it looks like you.

—Carl Gustav Horn

COMING SEPTEMBER 2007

Less than lucky but always plucky, costumed crimefighter Empowered returns for further misadventures, as a distress-prone girl wonder struggling with life on the superheroic C-list! Clad—or unclad, as fate would too often have it—in her embarrassingly revealing and maddeningly unreliable supersuit, she fights a never-ending battle against overly sensitive supervillains, irrationally envious superheroines, and her own body-image issues! Meanwhile, her boyfriend, Thugboy, plays with fire when he foolhardily attempts to compliment his profoundly insecure sweetheart on the awe-inspiring power of her . . . well, booty. And her often-inebriated gal-pal, Ninjette, pursues a drunken and ultimately disastrous mission to acquire Empowered some respect—by force if necessary! All this,

plus crossword-obsessed goons, speech-impaired superbeasts, "Ninjas Gone Wild," and even a few self-help hints from nigh-omnipotent cosmic overlords! You know, the usual.

From Adam Warren—writer/artist of the English-language *Dirty Pair* comics (the "Original English-Language Manga" that set the bar for all OEL) and writer of *Livewires*, *Gen13*, and *Iron Man: Hypervelocity* comes *Empowered*, a kickass long-john lampoon that flies to new heights of hotness and hilarity.

COMING OCTOBER 2007

Far in the future, humanity is locked in a seemingly endless war with a brutal alien race. The bloody conflict is dominated by giant war machines referred to as "Gear." Only the best and the brightest are allowed to drive these behemoths, and the process of elimination for pilots begins in junior high.

Thirteen-year-old Teresa Gottlieb has just entered the most prestigious military academy, known to all as Gear School, to try and become an elite Gear pilot. But on top of all the usual troubles that a seventh-grader has to put up with—boys, social cliques, hellish instructors—she also has to deal with three-story tall robots and an alien invasion!

Teresa needs to learn that when the bell rings, the adventure starts.

Gear School is written by Adam Gallardo (*Star Wars: Infinities—Return of the Jedi, 100 Girls*) and illustrated by Núria Peris (*Star Wars Tales, Karas*).

Teresa needs to learn that when the bell rings, **the adventure starts.**

SS SUBMISSIONS REQUIREMENTS

Here's your chance to get your artwork printed in *SS Magazine* in Japan, alongside the best in up-and-coming manga/anime/fantasy artists from around the world!

COLOR ILLUSTRATION SUBMISSIONS CORNER
SKY S

• Draw whatever you want, in any color medium!
• Size of artwork can be anywhere from postcard size (148mm x 100mm) to A4 (297mm x 210mm).

BLACK & WHITE ILLUSTRATION SUBMISSIONS CORNER
SEA S

• For "Sea S," draw whatever illustration you want!
• For "S Stage," draw any one-page comic you want. You can draw the one-page comic on a single postcard.
• "S Something" features four-panel comics focusing on your present life or interests.
• "S Story" features works that combine words and images. These are single pages that feature art as well as poetry, a monologue, or other text.
• "S Soul" features fan letters to *SS* contributors. You may receive an illustration as a gift!
• Size of artwork can be anywhere from postcard size (148mm x 100mm) to A4 (297mm x 210mm).

SUBMISSION REQUIREMENTS

Please include the following information on the back of your entry, and submit it to the appropriate category. (In the case of multiple entries, be sure to include the information on each one.)

1. Postal code, address, name, pseudonym, age, and phone number or e-mail address (contact info).
2. A few statements about the art.
3. Your previous magazine submissions history, and if you've appeared in *SS* before.

• Important Points
1. If your illustration is the type for which it is difficult to tell which side is up, left-right, etc., please specify on the back.
2. If you would like your artwork returned, please include a self-addressed envelope with sufficient return postage and write "Please Return" in red on the back of the art.
3. In the case of multiple entries, write the entry number of how many on the back of each illustration. (For example, if you send three illustrations, please label them 1/3, 2/3, and 3/3.)
4. The size of your submission can be anywhere from postcard to A4.
5. Please send CG works as printouts or send them digitally. In the case of e-mail submissions, please include all of the information listed above in your message. Please also see the details below for electronic submissions.

WHERE TO SEND YOUR ART

For electronic submissions:
• A picture resolution of 300dpi at actual size would be ideal. Any lower resolution might mean having to print at a smaller size in the magazine.
• When attaching the file to an e-mail, the data should be in compressed jpeg format no larger than 5MB. Any larger files should please be sent via file storage website.
• The address to send to is: ss@asukashinsha.co.jp

For mailed submissions:
c/o "SS [your category]", Asukashin Corp., Kanda #3 Amerex Building, 3-10 Jimbocho, Kanda, Chiyoda-ku, Tokyo 101-0051

COLOR ILLUSTRATIONS CAN BE BETWEEN POSTCARD AND A4 SIZE.
• Any smaller can only be reprinted small.

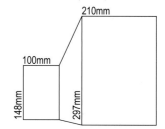

Postcard Size: Width 100mm, Height 148mm
A4 Size: Width 210mm, Height 297mm

FOR B&W ILLUSTRATIONS YOU CAN GO ANYWHERE FROM POSTCARD TO A4 SIZE.
• Any smaller can only be reprinted small.

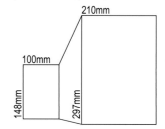

Postcard Size: Width 100mm, Height 148mm
A4 Size: Width 210mm, Height 297mm

"S STAGE" ONE-PAGE MANGA EXAMPLE
Please send submissions for "S Stage" on a postcard or board of similar size. Just split the card into panels and create your one-page manga as you would normally.

"S SOMETHING" FOUR-PANEL MANGA EXAMPLE
Submissions for "S Something" should be on a postcard or board of similar size split into four panels. Doing two strips on one card is also okay.

"S STORY" PICTURE AND PROSE EXAMPLE
Submissions for "S Story" should also be on a postcard or the like. The structure is up to you. In the example at left the picture is on top and words underneath, but the image could take up the whole page with words in the background, etc.